Assessment of Young Children

In an era of standards and norms where assessment tends to minimize or dismiss individual differences and results in punitive outcomes or no action at all, *Assessment of Young Children* provides teachers with an approach to assessment that is in the best interest of both children and their families. Author Lisa B. Fiore explores a variety of ways to study and assess young children in their natural environments, while stressing the importance of bringing children and families into the process. This lively text helps the reader learn how to cultivate developmentally appropriate practice, create appropriate expectations, examine children's work, interact in groups, and reflect upon their teaching practice. Accounts of real experiences from children, families, teachers, and administrators provide on-the-ground models of assessment strategies and demonstrate how children are affected.

Assessment of Young Children explores both standardized and authentic assessment, work sampling systems, and observation skills. Readers will walk away with strategies for communicating information about children and portfolio assessment, and understanding of how the use of formal and informal methods of observation, documentation, and assessment are connected to teacher and student inquiry. *Assessment of Young Children* encourages an assessment strategy where the child remains the focus, and explores how collaboration with children, families, and colleagues creates an image—not a diagnosis—of the child that is empowering, rather than constraining.

Special features include:
- Case study examples that anchor the concepts presented in the chapters and engage readers more deeply in the content.
- "Now What?" and "Avenues for Inquiry" throughout the book that present students with concrete extensions of the material that they may pursue for further investigation.

Lisa B. Fiore is an Associate Professor of Early Childhood Education and Dean of Faculty at Lesley University.

Assessment of Young Children

A Collaborative Approach

Lisa B. Fiore

 Routledge
Taylor & Francis Group

NEW YORK AND LONDON

KH

First published 2012
by Routledge
711 Third Avenue, New York, NY 10017

Simultaneously published in the UK
by Routledge
2 Park Square, Milton Park, Abingdon, Oxon OX14 4RN

Routledge is an imprint of the Taylor & Francis Group, an informa business

© 2012 Taylor & Francis

Library of Congress Cataloging-in-Publication Data
Fiore, Lisa B., 1970–
   Assessment of young children : a collaborative approach / Lisa B. Fiore.
      p. cm.
   Includes bibliographical references and index.
   I. Title.
   LB1139.23.F56 2012
   372.21–dc23   2011038839

ISBN: 978–0–415–88811–0 (hbk)
ISBN: 978–0–415–88812–7 (pbk)
ISBN: 978–0–203–83177–9 (ebk)

Typeset in Minion
by Swales & Willis Ltd, Exeter, Devon

Printed and bound in the United States of America

SFI Certified Sourcing
www.sfiprogram.org
SFI-00453

Printed and bound in the United States of America
by Edwards Brothers, Inc.

4/15/13

Dedication

This book is lovingly dedicated to Matthew, my champion, Talia, my mirth, and Steve, who took care of bedtime.

Contents

Figures

Tables

Preface

Italian educator Loris Malaguzzi (1920–94) believed that the education of young children should spring from children's own creativity and intrinsic desire to make meaning out of their world and their experiences in it. Credited with being a fundamental force behind the municipal schools that embody the globally renowned Reggio Emilia approach to early childhood education, Malaguzzi's words are often quoted as inspirational to early childhood educators. However, in a current educational climate that emphasizes assessment and accountability as primary, the notion that teachers and children share a desire "to do nothing without joy" runs counter to the realities that many teachers and children experience in classrooms—joy takes a back seat.

Effective early childhood teachers are aware that joy and learning are not at opposite ends of the teaching spectrum. Likewise, effective teachers recognize that children and families enter into the school as potential collaborators in the educational process—a process that is mutually beneficial to all who participate. All too often, and for many reasons, children and families are overlooked or discounted in efforts to gather data that will have a direct impact on the children's learning. This book provides a lens through which to examine a variety of ways to assess and study young children.

Assessment of Young Children: A Collaborative Approach is intended to examine a variety of ways to assess and study young children (ages 2–8, grades preK-2), and the underlying ideas that drive assessment. This book is also intended to challenge some assumptions (implicit and explicit) about early childhood education specifically, and teaching and learning more broadly. For example, one common assumption about education is as follows: a) teachers possess information, b) students do not possess this information, so c) teachers teach students what they do not know. Measuring the outcomes of this theorem involves subsequent assessment of what students know. In this scenario, teachers enter into the equation already knowing what students will know at the end of the journey.

Anyone who has ever traveled to a foreign or unfamiliar place has experienced the wonder of discovering something new and unexpected— following a path that wasn't indicated on a map just to see where it leads, trying to order dinner off a menu written in a totally different language. Taking risks and trusting in the capacity of others are not foreign concepts, yet these behaviors are endangered, as children and teachers are being taught that mistakes are bad and following one's curiosity or showing tremendous effort is not enough to succeed in school.

So why would a book about collaborative assessment be written by one individual? While there may be one author's name on the cover of this book, the work and stories contained between the covers is the result of much collaborative research, conversation, and observation. In this book, attention is given to developmentally appropriate practice and expectations, children's work, group interactions, and teacher behavior. This includes:

- establishing an image of the child as active, curious, and competent;
- inviting children and families into the assessment process;
- illustrating concepts through case studies and interactive web-based examples, which anchor material presented in chapters.

The case studies presented in this book are all based on actual examples communicated to or witnessed by the author. With the exception of the cases in Chapters 2 and 9, all case studies are fictional recreations. To ensure confidentiality, specific names and details have been changed. Each case study presents a scenario from the perspective of a particular individual invested in early childhood education, such as a child, parent, teacher, and administrator. Furthermore, summary questions at the end of each chapter provide readers with opportunities to actualize concepts and connect ideas to practice, thereby supporting deeper understanding and creative activity.

Ultimately, thoughtful and systematic investment in children and families will result in short-term and long-term gains for all citizens. As readers continue on their own journeys, they will be better able to participate as members of the early childhood education field armed with the knowledge that is constructed through the process of viewing assessment through a critical lens—one focused on children.

Acknowledgments

This book is the result of several years of conversations focused on the wellbeing of young children. Many of the stories contained within these chapters are drawn from the inspirational real-life work of very talented and insightful people. I wish to acknowledge Stephanie Cox Suarez, Karen Daniels, and Mikaela Newell for the work they do with young children and the difference they make in children's self-confidence and self-concepts. I also want to acknowledge Mary Geisser and Leslie Gleim, who are comfortable in uncharted territories and share children's joy and wonder in daily discoveries.

As this book evolved, the support and enthusiasm of several friends and colleagues had a tremendous impact on the writing. My thanks go out to Michael Pabian, who called at 7am from Seattle, and Stephen Gould, who dispenses with frivolities. My thanks also go to Suzanne Leone, Diane Ronchetti Cooper, and Rebecca Mason, for their perpetual laughter and inspirational stories. I would especially like to acknowledge Ben Mardell, a most generous teammate, kindred spirit, and partner in rubric revision. Working with Ben always improves the quality of my thinking, writing, and overall disposition.

Finally, I would like to thank my family for their patience and encouragement. Steve, Matthew, and Talia remind me daily of the importance of putting love front and center, and how collaboration makes learning more fun.

1

What Do You Notice?

When asked in an interview, 'How can we get back to schools which are places you go to learn?' Edgar Morin replied simply, "With love. And it is not my idea, I am simply quoting Plato." More than anything else children ask for attention and love.

(Vecchi, 2010, p. 27)

In an education climate marked by high-stakes testing, punitive measures for teachers and schools, and policies that sound and feel competitive by nature, after reading the above quote you may find yourself asking, "What's love got to do with it?" Tina Turner asked the same question in her 1984 hit song by the same name, and it boils down to a simple concept—relationships. These relationships include the relationships between and among children, teachers, families, community members, and government influence. Love is more or less visible in different, specific situations and examples, as assessment of young children contributes to the collective weaving of our nation's educational fabric.

Most early childhood teachers become teachers because of a fundamental love of learning and joy in sharing that passion with young children and like-minded colleagues. In terms of public education of our country's youngest citizens, the highest quality of human interaction in an early childhood classroom setting should be expected as a fundamental right on par with other rights outlined in our government structure—the right to free speech, religious practice, and interstate travel. Sounds simple. Yet you may have noticed that education today is anything but simple. Young children are impacted daily by teachers who are asked to adhere to a curriculum that is influenced by political and socio-cultural forces that greatly influence standards, expectations, and the image of children in the US. "Saying that our economic future rests on the success of our schools while ignoring the connection between our schools and the daily lives of people living in poverty is fundamentally dishonest" (Coleman-Kiner, 2011, p. 25). Somewhere along the accountability pathway, love often takes a backseat to outcomes and benchmarks, leaving pre-service teachers, novice teachers, and veterans alike to wonder, "How did we get here?"

A Closer Look at Accountability

Identity and assessment are at the heart of the issue and related confusion about accountability. It will be helpful to gain a sense of the current educational landscape before we begin to address assessment, specifically. First, American public schools are currently caught in a societal knot as educators and legislators grapple with the role of education. This is not a new knot—indeed our country has been struggling with the role of education for decades. In my yellowed copy of *Radical school reform* (Gross & Gross, 1969), I recently re-read the editors' introduction. The editors contextualize the critics' appraisals of schools, stating, "What they find in the classroom is suppression, irrelevance, inhumanity, manipulation, and the systematic stultification of most of what is promising in children and youth" (p. 17).

Over forty years later, Diane Ravitch writes of her involvement in the school reform efforts of the 1990s and early 2000s, in *The death and life of the great American school system* (2010), stating her concern:

> that accountability, now a shibboleth that everyone applauds, had become mechanistic and even antithetical to good education. Testing, I realized with dismay, had become a central preoccupation in the schools and was not just a measure but an end in itself . . . [Accountability] was not raising standards but dumbing down the schools as states and districts strived to meet unrealistic targets.
>
> (pp. 12–13)

So what is a realistic target for children, families, educators and policy-makers to aim for and agree upon? "It is almost as if we are afraid to say that our work is a purely human endeavor—that our jobs are to develop human beings" (Coleman-Kiner, 2011, p. 25). Young children are born citizens, and will be the citizens of the future who will determine the solvency of our nation. Is the role of education to transmit culture or to construct culture? Depending on the stance taken, accountability drives assessment that looks and feels quite different from the perspective of children, families, teachers, and policy-makers.

Some argue that schools are places to transmit culture, with particular effort made to close cultural gaps that lead to academic inequities (Wilson & Weiner, 2001). These cultural gaps (e.g. the achievement gap, the school-readiness gap) are typically linked to socio-economic gaps, namely poverty, and the benefits of quality early childhood programs are targeted at reducing our country's high dropout rate. Yet an emphasis on school reform rather than increased, pervasive social services tends to dominate mainstream media attention.

Maintaining the cultural transmission stance often means that schools are places where teachers are responsible for preserving culture, transmitted through standards based curricula and monitored using traditional assessment. When only one out of every ten American kindergarteners living in low-income environments becomes a college graduate (Darling-Hammond, 2010), the US education system clearly will not be able to compete on a global scale. If public education is the responsibility of American citizens, then accountability viewed through this lens fuels the competitive fire that drives many politicians and public policy in the cultural transmission stance.

Others posit that schools are places where culture is constantly renewed and reconstructed by those who participate in the classrooms. Dewey (1916) believed that learning is an inherent part of the teaching process, and more recent scholarship supports the notion of accountability as a multifaceted construct, rather than a one-dimensional, unidirectional goal (Krechevsky, Rivard, & Burton, 2010). In 2005, the National Association of Elementary School Principals (NAESP) Foundation developed a guide for leaders of early childhood learning communities, featuring six standards illustrated in Figure 1.1. Maintaining this stance means that schools are places where

> [l]earning and knowledge are therefore made possible . . . by the interaction between individuals who are building knowledge along with others, and their physical and cultural environment. The individual and the context thus take on substance. They define each other and give each other identity.
>
> (Strozzi, 2001, p. 58)

Assessment and accountability in this vein are multi-dimensional, incorporating multiple perspectives and media to demonstrate the learning that occurs within a particular context.

A Closer Look at Assessment

The attempt to strike a delicate balance, between cultural transmission and construction, is perhaps experienced most acutely by teachers. Teachers frequently grapple with a tension between pedagogy that is thoughtfully designed according to a set of values and beliefs about what

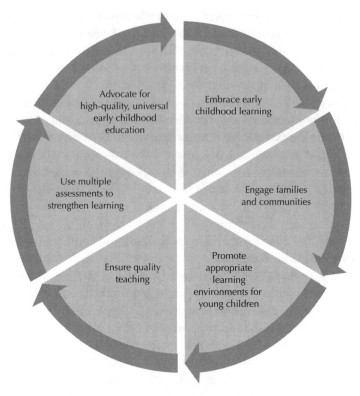

Figure 1.1 Standards for Leaders of Early Childhood Learning Communities

Adapted from NAESP, 2005.

is appropriate for young children, and policies that demand specific academic results according to measures that teachers don't necessarily perceive as valid indicators of children's abilities. I frequently hear student teachers, in the midst of their student teaching placements, complaining that the idealism with which they entered their placement settings (e.g. hopes and passion for children's and their own learning) is being challenged by the realities of classroom demands (e.g. "canned" curriculum, excessive requirements). Although teaching and assessment are inextricably linked, teaching and testing are often hard to reconcile.

Assessment and testing have become synonymous terms, when in fact their meanings, applications, and implications are quite distinct. Although there are many different definitions of assessment and testing, some distinguishing features include the following:

- Assessment is often a process that includes information gained from many different childhood experiences and activities, while testing is typically limited to a particular instrument with a specific goal.

- Assessment often includes input from multiple sources and collaborators, such as parents and guardians, administrators, service providers, advocates, and legislators, while testing is typically limited to information contributed by the individual test-taker without any requisite feedback once the test is completed.
- Assessment may occur in formal and informal settings, using various techniques, while testing requires specific, explicit directions to be followed in order to believe that the data is scientifically sound.
- Assessment framed in terms of evaluation and understanding often feels better to early childhood professionals than testing that is linked to numerical scores (and related anxiety and job security) and more structured class time.

For the purposes of dialogue generated from the reading of this book, the ideal early childhood assessment is a process that includes and/or results in products that inform decisions made about children and curriculum. The process is informed by others and is rooted in developmentally appropriate activities for children aged 2–8.

In current early childhood classrooms, most assessment is designed to acquire information that will help responsible individuals make decisions in the interest of a child's growth and development. Testing as part of such assessment takes time and resources, and a larger number of children in a particular class means more time and resources are required to administer and evaluate the testing. This mandatory time either reduces classroom time for free play and exploration or must be carved out of other organized periods of the day, such as recess, lunchtime, or "specials" (art, music, library). The assessment process is further challenging because teachers recognize that one particular test or score does not paint a full, clear picture of a complex, developing child. This is supported by research that states that standardized testing of children under the age of 8 is scientifically invalid and contributes to detrimental labeling that can permanently damage a child's educational future (Miller & Almon, 2009). Yet the pressures to incorporate more assessment into an increasingly academically focused day continue.

Effects of Accountability and Assessment

The ripple effects of school, state, and national pressures can be felt at every level of the education system, from early childhood education through higher education and the accompanying administrative offices. Currently, and for reasons that will be articulated in Chapter 4, a public school district is held accountable for students' progress as evidenced by the scores produced by students in its schools. Likewise, a teacher education program that claims to educate early childhood teachers may be held accountable if graduates can't demonstrate that their students are meeting standards required by the town, state, or the US. The cycle of accountability indeed captures all levels of education, yet we must be careful that the responsibility with which we imbue teachers is reasonable and ethical. Recent reports posing allegations against Superintendent Beverly Hall in the Atlanta, GA school district (see Vogell, 2011) describe a culture of fear and pressure that can prompt well-intentioned citizens to question and suspend ethics, and the extreme lengths that educators may go to to convince others that achievement is possible, despite demographic odds (e.g. race, financial security).

Attempts to diminish the perceived weight of standardized assessments have evolved in recent years, yet standardized measures are being required of children in younger grades, such as preschool. Alternative assessments, such as "performance-based assessment," grew out of a desire by many educators to offer measurable hands-on tasks that differ from traditional standardized tests. In early childhood classrooms, examples of children's work demonstrate knowledge and understanding through application:

- drawing a picture of an American scientist on a self-designed postage stamp;
- writing a haiku poem about your family;
- acting out a scene from a story;
- composing a song about caterpillars.

In the higher education arena, however, performance-based assessment is two-tiered. It is conducted by gathering samples of adult students' work in the higher education setting, and also extending the assessment into the classroom settings in which the adult students teach—gathering samples from those children (pupils). The idea is that institutions of higher education should be held accountable for their graduates' ability to produce desirable results (e.g. high test scores, strong writing samples) in their classrooms. If higher performance of young children is desired, then a complex solution is needed. Such a solution requires the coordination of many people, many minds, many dollars, and much patience. This book is not intended to provide a detailed economic analysis of our country's education system, but will instead offer guidance and suggested resources that might serve as provocation for further investigation and dialogue with others. Some significant "others" that are critical to sustained, dynamic conversations about early childhood assessment are children and families.

Early childhood teachers encounter parents' questions daily, and these questions usually originate from a place of concern—concern from a caregiver for his or her child's current and future success in school and life. What caregivers see occurring in a classroom may not clearly reveal the thoughtful curriculum planning and consideration for social and emotional competence that lies beneath the surface. When Early Intervention specialists and home visitors in Early Head Start settings—those who work with children and families in the earliest months and years of children's lives—increasingly receive questions such as, "But what is my child *learning*? Why is she only *playing*?" it is clear that a misperception exists. In this scenario, knowledge (valued and critical for future success) and play (nice, but not as important) are at opposing ends of a learning spectrum. This book is intended to serve as a compass that will:

- guide readers who wish to learn more about assessment of young children;
- empower readers to examine and develop observation, documentation, and assessment skills and strategies that serve multiple, mutually beneficial goals;
- support readers in efforts to invite others (family members, colleagues, service providers) into the assessment process as collaborators who inform an image of an individual child or group of young children in a classroom context.

Noticing

One of the primary ideas underlying classroom assessment can be captured in a succinct question—"What do you notice?" This question is enough to propel and sustain inquiry into a host of topics. From a child's standpoint, she might notice that yellow and blue, when mixed together, make green. From a teacher's perspective, she might notice that a child enjoys experimenting with colors of paint. The distinction between the child's and teacher's respective "noticing" is quite important. The child may be satisfied with the result of the accident or scientific experiment that results in a new discovery about color. The teacher's noticing, however, may lead to subsequent questions about a child's skills and knowledge. The teacher can use observation and recording strategies to:

- follow a child's progress;
- gauge whether a new discovery was accidental or the result of newly acquired hypotheses about materials and their properties;

- see if and how the knowledge transfers to other classroom centers and content;
- consider how this assessment will inform classroom instruction.

The teacher's job is to constantly consider how to accurately measure an individual child in the classroom and use the results in a way that extends and informs subsequent curriculum design, implementation, and assessment for individuals and the group as a whole. The teacher's role and responsibility are critical factors in any meaningful relationship between the assessment, any intervention strategies or plan, and evaluation of the assessment. Sometimes this process begins with noticing, and that noticing leads to the desire to find answers to some fundamental questions relating to children's learning—Why? Who? When? How? and What?

Why? The Seeds of Inquiry

Effective early childhood teachers routinely wish to learn more about the "Why" that precedes (and often perpetuates) a child's actions and behavior. As mentioned earlier in this chapter, early childhood teachers are drawn to the profession because of a deep love of learning and sharing that passion with young children. Despite pressures relating to assessment and accountability, or perhaps because of those pressures, early childhood teachers consistently examine the children with whom they work and learn and play.

The notion of teacher as researcher will be discussed in the final chapter of this book, as a bookend of sorts to this first chapter that sets the stage for a certain disposition toward teaching and learning with young children. Marilyn Cochran-Smith and Susan Lytle state, in the preface to their book *Inquiry as stance* (2009), that the "knowledge needed for teachers to teach well and to enhance students' learning opportunities and life chances [can] not be generated solely by researchers . . . centrally positioned outside of schools" (p. vii). When teachers think of themselves as researchers and scientists, and conduct their work in a similar vein as the students they teach, they are generating hypotheses in a spirit of curiosity and inquiry. These efforts naturally lend themselves to ongoing, rigorous assessment and evaluation of students that is refined with practice and experience.

When teachers notice something that they wish to examine further, the seeds of inquiry have been planted. The seeds of inquiry are actually data, and as such can be thought of as catalysts of activity. Data is (and are) defined as facts or factual information, and facts are not necessarily static, unchanging bits of information. What appears one way in one situation may look quite different in another situation.

Take a child who chooses to sit alone and draw during choice time on Tuesday morning. An observer in the classroom on that day may gather observational data that leads him to wonder whether or not the child is on par socially with her peers, due to the lack of interaction she displayed with other children. The next day, the same child may lead a group of classmates in fantasy play in the block-building area, in which pirates are attacking the ship they've built. It has been stated that "[c]ollecting data should be preceded by planning how the data will be used, who should have access to them, in what decisions they will play a role, and what stakeholders need to know about them," (Snow & Van Hemel, 2008, p. 3). Arguably, thoughtful planning is a personal and professional skill that serves an important purpose. And yet sometimes data happens, and the teacher's responsibility is to notice and act accordingly.

Knowing how to respond to data that is purposefully gathered or inadvertently attained boils down to a common core principle: early childhood teachers must possess a strong knowledge of child development. This knowledge serves as a backdrop against which children are measured, formally and informally, in effective practice. Children who are between the ages of 2 and 8 years old have physical, cognitive, and social skills and needs that differ dramatically from those of older children. Furthermore, development occurs quickly in the early years of life, so recognizing typical versus unusual behavior is important for both curriculum development and intervention, as warranted. This means that a teacher needs to be mindful of where a child is developmentally at a given point in time, and where the child is expected to be at a future date. Accurate and developmentally appropriate assessment has the potential to significantly impact an individual child's current and future academic experiences, as well as evolving images of herself as a learner and a citizen. If a goal of education is to improve children's learning, then better teaching is key, but not enough (Parr & Timperley, 2008).

Who? Examining the Learning Group

The focus on individual learning and assessment in American schools supports the idea that independence and autonomy are important goals. This is a bit tricky to reconcile and understand in today's classrooms, since conformity to established standards and desired outcomes dominates much of teachers' time and the curriculum offered. On the one hand, autonomy has been part of the fabric of American history since our nation's inception. However, it was the collaborative efforts of many minds and bodies that resulted in *The Declaration of Independence* and *Constitution*. Similar collaborative efforts occur daily in early childhood classrooms—in the block corner, at snack time, and during recess—with impact perhaps less grand but no less powerful to the players. Early Americans desired to be free from English rule, and to accept responsibility for their own survival and prosperity. Responsibility and prosperity involved sacrifice then, and it appears the same can be said today.

> These tests are the coin of the realm. Based on test scores, schools can be sanctioned or even closed, children uprooted, jobs lost, and mayoral elections decided. Reputations of principals, superintendents, and state commissioners of educations are determined, on large measure, by test scores.
>
> (Mardell, Fiore, Boni, & Tonachel, 2010, p. 41)

If the primary assessment target is the individual child, then the teacher is often required to have tunnel vision and tune out the influence of others on an individual child's thinking and behavior. Therefore the relationships noted at the beginning of the chapter, so critical to children's learning, are often not valued in the same way as evidence of academic progress. The teacher must take "an inherently group setting—school—and try to individualize it" despite the fact that "the types of activities, available materials, and time frame for working are often the same for all children in the class" (Krechevsky & Mardell, 2001, p. 284).

When a teacher shifts her perspective to view herself and the students in her classroom as a learning group, rather than merely a collection of individuals, the classroom becomes one more closely aligned with democratic principles such as social engagement and citizenship. "A small group with a big purpose—in terms of learning and in terms of producing—enlarges the significance of the group, but, paradoxically, does not reduce the significance of the individual" (Seidel, 2001, p. 312). It will be helpful to articulate what distinguishes a learning group from any group, particularly with respect to early childhood education and assessment that is a collaborative effort.

A provocative conceptualization of learning groups has been suggested by Krechevsky & Mardell (2001), and is illustrated in Table 1.1. Adult members of a learning group can include teachers, families and other family members, and other school staff and service providers. This inclusive approach is consistent with the inclusive practices of, for example, team assessment such as writing and implementing Individualized Education Plans (as will be discussed in Chapter 8). The primary difference is that learning is co-constructed and shared by all

Table 1.1 Four Features of Learning Groups

- The members of learning groups include adults as well as children.
- Documenting children's learning processes helps to make learning visible and shapes the learning that takes place.
- Members of learning groups are engaged in the emotional and aesthetic as well as the intellectual dimensions of learning.
- The focus of learning in learning groups extends beyond the learning of individuals to create a collective body of knowledge.

Source: Krechevsky & Mardell (2001, p. 286).

members of the group, instead of a few members demonstrating learning while other members measure and evaluate the learning. Assessment in this case is very much part of the culture of the classroom, but the power dynamic (e.g. who holds the power and the knowledge) looks and feels dramatically different.

Consider documentation, for example. Documentation of children's learning takes many forms, and there are many educators around the world actively engaged in documentation practices that include the use of photographs, video clips, samples of students' work, and narratives. (Note: The *Avenues for Inquiry* section at the end of this chapter provides some websites that feature documentation that may inspire some innovative practices of your own.) The following case study will serve as our first example of others that you will find throughout this book—concrete links between ideas and classroom application. As you read the case study and after you have read it, consider what strikes you as significant. Your interpretation may differ greatly from that of someone else, which can open up some interesting dialogue. There is no one right way to draw meaning from the case study; rather, as you consider various viewpoints, you will gain a sense of how assessment informs teaching and learning.

Case Study: The Wonder of Documentation

Mrs. Babylon and Ms. Kriss co-teach a kindergarten class of twenty-six 5-year-olds in Boston, MA. Last spring, when they prepared to launch their curriculum unit on Heroes, they designated one wall of their classroom as the documentation wall, where they would use documentation as both a reflective tool to revisit learning with the children, and also as a timeline to display the next steps in their group's learning process. The documentation wall was a new addition to the already familiar places in the classroom, such as the Word Wall/Literacy area, Math/Science area, and Dramatic Play space. They spent several planning sessions discussing how they would display photos, narrative descriptions, and samples of students' work from left to right, as someone would read a book.

The two teachers decided that the "hook" they would use to engage the children in their topic was superheroes. They therefore chose a suitable children's comic book to be their initial core text. For the first few days, the children explored the comic book and the teachers took photos of the children reading. Children drew pictures of their own superheroes, and the class discussed the process (thought process as well as representational process) of drawing superheroes. Some topics raised in class discussions were: what resources are needed to create the product; the use of colors to represent different virtues; and costumes and symbols. The teachers used photographs, samples of children's work, and snippets from discussions to remind children of their previous ideas and work.

To build on the children's excitement, the teachers decided to introduce the children to a superhero, "Green Wonder" (Ms. Kriss in full costume), who came into the classroom and talked with the children about her powers and how she happened to lose them. During the discussion it was decided that over the next month the children would interview Green Wonder about her powers before and after she lost them, and they divided the topic into body powers, brain powers, and caring powers.

**

A local radio show host, who happened to be a parent of a child in the kindergarten, was invited to the classroom one day as an "interview expert" for this unit. "Your teachers invited me to share some skills with you, which I use in my job everyday when I interview different people," the parent told the class. He talked about key questions to ask in any interview—Who? What? When? Where? How?—and the children practiced writing their own questions during Writer's Workshop and other free times during the day. Teachers put samples of children's questions on the documentation wall over the course of several days and analyzed them with the children. The group noted how early questions such as, "What were your powers that you lost?" had changed to "What would you rather like to have back, your heat vision or flight?" The level of detail in their questions had clearly become more sophisticated.

**

Throughout the unit, children's ideas about their own superhero personalities had bubbled up in conversations, drawings, and writing. Mrs. Babylon and Ms. Kriss decided to shift their focus from the interview to the children creating their own superheroes. Children designed uniforms that identified specific skills that they possessed. For instance, one child designed a rainbow-colored emblem because she wanted her superhero "to be able to make fighting people happy." Other color schemes featured "red, orange, and yellow like fire" and "blue like the ocean," and children decided upon names for their self-designed heroes. The process of choosing names led to discussions about the features of names and initials. Noting the connections to content areas, the teachers communicated with families and administrators (using weekly newsletters and a class website) about how their superhero investigation was leading to greater phonemic awareness, as evident in children's learning about letter sounds and initials, and applied math and social studies skills, as evident in their cityscape design and mural.

The teachers told the class about something that they had noticed during their observations of children's conversations—comic book stories typically occur in urban settings. The teachers invited a "mural expert" from the Museum of Fine Arts to talk with the class about cityscapes. They practiced drawing cities of their own, working toward a class mural that would depict a cityscape in which their superheroes lived. The teachers and children measured their individual drawings and thought about placement of the images, such as how much space would be needed for one child's super vehicle and how long a building would need to be to represent it true to scale. In one circle time the class looked at artifacts on their documentation wall, and the discussion expanded to include the process of building cities and what the children knew about cities (e.g. needing protection and help running cities).

***

Everyone in the class was very invested in their individual and group work around superheroes, and every week Mrs. Babylon suggested that they look at their class's documentation up to that point to review their group's journey from the beginning of the superhero work to the current time. Simple prompts such as, "How did we decide to paint the building here gray?" sparked a lively conversation as children remembered their learning process. As they looked at their cityscape, one child suggested that they all add their own superheroes to the cityscape mural. "What do we need to do to make this big paper look like an illustration in a comic book?" asked Mrs. Babylon.

Children's ideas included "super postures"—physical positions that superheroes often assume when they're acting powerful—and thought and speech bubbles that conveyed what the superheroes

Figure 1.2
Superhero Play
at Home

were communicating to the reader and other superheroes. As the children added pictures of their superhero-selves to the cityscape, they learned about onomatopoeia with examples such as "Pow!" "Bam!" and "Hiss!" that were associated with bravery and other actions. Several parents commented informally that their children were "playing superheroes at home" and that they seemed "to know so much about comic books and hero themes." One parent was motivated to seek out his childhood comic book collection from the attic and share it with his child.

***

These experiences contributed to a common knowledge base constructed by the children, teachers, families, and guests. Mrs. Babylon and Ms. Kriss decided to help the group transition from fictional to real-life heroes by having Green Wonder come in for a final visit. "Can you think of people in your community who are community helpers?" asked Green Wonder. She explained that while her powers aren't real there are people in the community who use powers every day to help make the city run smoothly and safely. The children identified police officers as examples of real-life heroes who use their brain, body, and caring powers everyday to help people, and Mrs. Babylon invited a female police officer to the class as their final guest expert for the unit.

Using their newly refined interview skills, the children interviewed Officer Mason about her work and the tools she uses daily that help her do her job. The class took field trips to the local post office and fire department to gather information about tools other people use in their work. They recorded their information on "note-catcher sheets" that were placed on the documentation wall, which had been cleared to focus on the new non-fiction angle of their investigation. Photos, narratives, and samples of students' work filled the wall in the same way other artifacts had in previous weeks.

The unit culminated with an Open House night. The children chose whether or not to wear their superhero capes (they all wore them!) and posed for photos with family and friends in front of the cityscape. Each child picked three pieces of learning that they wanted to share with their families, and these were compiled in a class comic book titled, "Superheroes can . . ." that Mrs. Babylon printed and distributed to all of the visitors. The final documentation wall was about reflection and review. The wall was divided into panels like a comic book, with each panel telling a story about their learning process.

The children and adults depicted in the preceding case study benefitted from the systematic use of documentation (e.g. photos, samples of children's work) to extend and enhance the learning for all of the individual members of the group. This type of practice affords teachers numerous opportunities to:

- assess children's learning using informal and formal methods;
- engage parents and other experts;
- balance what they know with what they desire to know over time.

The concept of time is particularly relevant in the section that follows. Assessments, like human development, are most effective when certain key factors are aligned in an appropriate context.

When? Developmentally Appropriate Practice

The most appropriate assessment strategies and tools to promote children's learning and teacher effectiveness must coordinate with the most appropriate developmental period in order for maximum learning to occur. In other words, assessments such as standardized tests are not always suitable for young children aged 2–8. As mentioned at the beginning of the chapter, there has been much recent research to support the idea that tests used to predict children's future academic outcomes are not reliable for a host of reasons. Some complicating factors include a child's personality or mood, the type of test offered, test content, testing conditions, and variations in any of these factors among the assessment group (MIELL, 2010). Because young children are often located in a variety of settings (at home, family center, group center, public school) before they enter formal education classrooms, the concept of accurate or useful assessments is further complicated.

Some efforts to guide assessment strategies and to encourage developmentally appropriate practices have been led by experts in the field of early childhood education. The National Association for the Education of Young Children (NAEYC), a highly regarded non-profit organization in the US, which focuses on early childhood education professionals and policies, published a joint position statement in which *developmentally appropriate practices* are defined as those that consider both age (chronological development) and individual qualities (e.g. personality, family/culture, learning style) as viewed through a knowledge-of-child-development lens (NAEYC, 2003).

If teachers are experts in child development and know the children in their classrooms well, then they should know the best means of assessing what the children know and where and how the children can demonstrate progress. However, the tension discussed earlier with regard to accountability often prohibits teachers' knowledge from entering into formal assessments. Objectivity (discussed in detail in Chapter 4) is seen as desirable from a standardized (and norm-referenced) testing standpoint, because objective measures are designed to ensure that there is as little bias and variability as possible to uphold scientific standards.

Here's the topsy-turvy part—research has shown that "[o]nly someone with ongoing, subjective knowledge of the child, who has witnessed the child's activities across multiple contexts, can accurately assess which skills are a legitimate part of a child's repertoire" (MIELL, 2010, p. 4). Who are the people who are most subjective and witness children in multiple contexts? Teachers and family members. Although the term *stakeholders* has been used to refer to individuals and groups with an investment in children's education, teachers and family members do not appear to carry equal weight in determining the most appropriate means of assessing young children. The current business model of education places teachers' jobs at risk if children do not show adequate growth, and yet most of children's development is out of teachers' control.

How? Considering Assessment Methods and Tools

The concept of developmentally appropriate practice is multi-dimensional (Copple & Bredekamp, 2009), which lends support to the idea that assessment should consider multiple dimensions as well. In fact, there is much to consider. First and foremost, the goals of assessment and the strengths and weaknesses of specific methods and tools need to be considered with regard to the goals of individual schools and accountability pressures. The methods and content in any assessment are most effective when they align with children's interests, behaviors, and abilities, and standardized test procedures do not necessarily mean that children will respond in a standardized fashion. For example, if an assessment tool is designed with limited room for visible growth over time, a child may make academic progress in the classroom over time, but the progress may not be measured accurately using that specific tool.

Authentic assessment (to be discussed in Chapter 5) often complements standardized assessment or provides an alternative to standardized measures that sometimes result in the mismeasurement of young children. Authentic assessment, such as observation, typically features children engaged in ordinary activities, multiple perspectives from several individual adults/professionals, and flexibility to accommodate children's needs and familiarity with materials. When children are removed from their classrooms to be tested, they are instantly out of their element, in unfamiliar surroundings, looking at and responding to questions out of context. This makes many teachers as uncomfortable as the children. Therefore the passion and joy that steers people into an early childhood profession is often associated with authentic assessment, because it is anchored in child development and recognizes the influence of the environment on children's learning. And yet there are benefits of standardized assessment measures that lead to successful interventions and support for many young children and families.

Table 1.2 illustrates some teacher and/or parent "noticings." These initial noticings are listed next to possible assessment methods and potential collaborators with whom to access and evaluate information. This process would inform decisions about curriculum, as well as cognitive and social development.

Used well, both standardized and authentic assessments inform families, educators, administrators, and the general public about information that can be used to promote what is best for the future of young children, and indeed all citizens.

What? What Does it All Mean?

> If the school for young children has to be preparatory and provide continuity with the elementary school, then we as educators are already prisoners of a model that ends up as a funnel . . . Its purpose is to narrow down what is big into what is small. This choking device is against nature. If you put it upside down, it serves no purpose.
>
> (Malaguzzi, 1998, p. 88)

Table 1.2 Noticing, Questions, and Collaborative Assessment

Noticing & Questions	Assessment Methods	Collaborators
A small group of 3-year-olds has been rolling round objects down a long wooden block that is propped up to serve as a ramp. *What do the children know about physics, and how can I extend their learning through provocation and the sharing of documentation?*	Observations of the group's play; photos and/or video of the group engaged in this activity; review of developmental guidelines and experiences suggested for this age group; review of science and technology standards for young children.	Fellow teacher, assistant, or parent. Children in the class.
In her kindergarten classroom, Hana has been involved in several conflicts with peers and seeks out adult attention. Her family is anticipating the birth of her baby sister soon. *Is Hana's aggression and desire for adult companionship typical from a developmental perspective? What materials can I bring into the classroom (e.g. dramatic play area, book corner) to support Hana as she anticipates the arrival of her new sibling and subsequent changes in her family?*	Observations of Hana during group activities; photos and/or video of Hana engaged with peers and adults; interview with parents; developmental screening/checklist.	Fellow teacher, assistant, school psychologist, art therapist, expressive therapist.
Isaiah asks to be excused to use the bathroom every day during his 2nd grade class's math time. *Is Isaiah confused by the math concepts or terminology being taught? Is he mastering the knowledge required according to state standards?*	Samples of Isaiah's math work; comparison of assessment scores to curriculum goals and assessment benchmarks; discussion with Isaiah about math concepts using story or music instead of math worksheets; photos or video of Isaiah during math time.	Fellow teacher, assistant, Isaiah, district math coach or curriculum director.

So what does all of the information in this chapter mean for teachers, families, and others who are committed to providing children with rich early childhood education experiences? What can teachers of young children do to ensure that school is a place of "purpose"—where the "big ideas" Malaguzzi alluded to in the above quote are in synch with, not at odds with, the role of schools in the United States?

The answers to these questions are not simple, which is why the collaborative emphasis in this book is so critical for the future of young children and education. In order for early childhood assessment to be meaningful for young children, it needs to relate to them developmentally, culturally, and academically. For teachers, early childhood assessment is complicated by their responsibilities to self, to children and families, and to the schools in which they teach—schools often pressured to produce evidence of students' learning in order to receive funding and job security. When the purpose of education is fueled by economic incentives, as it is currently, the focus on organic "big ideas" is narrowed to measurable outcomes.

If public education is a public resource, then public investment seems logical. Some argue that while the "social rate of return" on public investments (a.k.a., money) in education is high in terms of the life-long "well-being" of children, businesses may not see their potential gains as worthy of the investment, because the short-term returns aren't currently as appealing, or visible, as more lucrative investments (Folbre, 2011). Systematic documentation of children's learning would make visible the gains children make in literacy or math, for example, and would also communicate strengths inherent in different approaches to problem-solving, creativity, and diversity.

Recently, the US government has proposed a large investment in early childhood education—the $500 million Race to the Top-Early Learning Challenge. Although there is both praise and criticism related to the plan and the links to the K-12 public education system (see Kagan & Kauerz, 2011), this is a collaborative effort between two government organizations (Department of Education and Department of Health and Human Services) that have never before joined forces in the interest of building and sustaining systems that support young children. If the collaboration inspires other collaborative efforts between practitioners, institutions of higher education, social service organizations, and other for- and not-for-profit organizations in countless combinations, then assessment and accountability can help shape both policy and practice.

"Boosting social capital and human capital—competence, confidence, and connections—makes it more likely that youngsters will succeed" (Kirp, 2011, p. 173). Relationships between caring individuals from different areas of influence *can* affect significant, sustainable practices in early childhood classrooms. Assessment and investment *can* work together, and this requires communication among the so-called stakeholders so that the expertise that each group or individual brings to the process is utilized, respected, and translated into action on behalf of our youngest citizens.

Summary

In this chapter you've been encouraged to think about early childhood assessment as a complex process that has relationships at its core—relationships between children, families, teachers and practitioners, content (subject matter and materials) and the environment. The current political climate is one in which accountability for students' learning extends from early childhood classrooms to higher education classrooms, and beyond to the policy and legislation arenas. Teachers often experience a tension between using developmentally appropriate practices and assessments and using tools targeted at measuring desired outcomes, despite a potential mismatch with children's developmental levels. As a result of reading about the core questions that can stem from noticing children's behaviors and the need for accurate assessments that can promote learning for all young children, you should be able to view early childhood assessment through a more critical lens—critical because as citizens: 1) we should thoughtfully evaluate benefits and weaknesses in current assessment procedures and related consequences; 2) we are poised at a critical time for early childhood education due to political attention and potential alliances; and 3) we are parts of a greater whole that is enriched through collaboration.

Now What?

1. Consider need for accountability in early childhood settings. How do you explain the potential value of assessment? Think of an example in your own life and describe how assessment informed your educational experience. Do you think the process helped you to learn or develop more?
2. Several issues were presented that thread their way through early childhood assessment, such as politics, economics, and competition. Why do you think these are prevalent issues? Examine each one separately and defend your reasons for stating that each has strong developmental implications.
3. Throughout the chapter, the important role that collaboration plays was stressed. What do you think of this emphasis? Think about your own life and the influences that teachers, family members, and others have had in your own educational experience, and cite those in your answer.

Avenues for Inquiry

The Alliance for Childhood

This organization is an excellent resource for policies and practices that focus on children's healthy development and key qualities such as love of learning and joy in daily life.
http://www.allianceforchildhood.org

The National Association for the Education of Young Children

A professional organization that emphasizes excellence in early childhood education settings. Information is available for practitioners and care-givers, and annual conference and professional development offerings are featured.
http://www.naeyc.org

Project Zero at Harvard Graduate School of Education

This website has documentation of children's learning at its core, featuring examples of individual and group learning from early childhood classrooms and other educational contexts. Explicit connections to Project Zero and collaboration with educators in Reggio Emilia, Italy are presented through links and projects.
http://pzweb.harvard.edu/mlv/

2

Role of the Environment

> The environment is a powerful educating force, in and of itself, and everything about it sends strong messages to the children who live there.
>
> (Felstiner, 2004, p. 41)

Now that the stage has been set to consider assessment of young children through a collaborative lens, we can begin to examine some of the major influences on assessment, beginning with something that is often over-looked as having a significant impact on children and families—the environment. For the purposes of this chapter, we will consider several settings that comprise learning environments for young children. These settings function independently as discrete systems nested within the other (as illustrated in Figure 2.1), but also interact over time.

The environments in Figure 2.1 interact in more and less obvious ways. For example, a city or town may influence a school in terms of its property or resources available to hire highly qualified teachers. Likewise, a kindergarten class's investigation into sustainability and "going green" can change a school's recycling policy and purchasing practices, and trickle into families' homes and the larger community. Individuals committed to the healthy and successful development of young children recognize the need to design and sustain environments for young children that are accessible, functional, and safe, while at the same time visually pleasing, welcoming, and nurturing.

It is important to note that while I strongly believe a child's home environment plays a more significant role than other environmental systems, I am glad that the home environment is not a primary context in which assessment of the sort discussed in this text occurs. From the standpoint of collaboration, the home best serves as a rich source of information that can inform and complement educational assessment efforts. In a highly significant study that summarized a vast body of child development research, the authors note that, "The essential features of

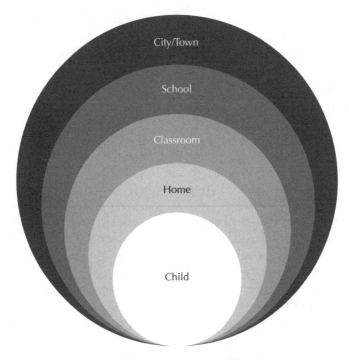

City/Town

School

Classroom

Home

Child

Figure 2.1 Learning Environments and the Young Child

the environment that influence children's development are their relationships with the important people in their lives . . . within the places to which they are exposed—from playgrounds to libraries to schools to soccer fields" (National Scientific Council on the Developing Child, 2004, p. 4).

When environments are thoughtfully designed for young children, they are developmentally appropriate and welcoming to families. Aspects of environments for 3-year-olds will be different than aspects of environments for 8-year-olds. This is to be expected, although there are some desirable qualities that all educational environments can share, such as an environment's "power to organize, promote pleasant relationships among people of different ages, create a handsome environment, provide changes, promote choices and activity, and its potential for sparking all kinds of social, affective, and cognitive learning" (Loris Malaguzzi, quoted in Gandini, 1998, p. 177).

Some educators have stated that environments function as partners "in the teaching-learning process" (Scheinfeld, Haigh, & Scheinfeld, 2008, p. 71). Educators in Reggio Emilia, Italy share a similar opinion of the environment "as educating the child; in fact it is considered as 'the third teacher' along with the team of two teachers" (Gandini, 1998, p.177). If the environment is viewed as a teacher of young children, then it bears some of the same responsibilities as a teacher, such as contributing to ongoing, informative assessment that promotes children's learning and development. As we begin to explore classroom, school, and community environments, consider the mutually reciprocal influence that the environment and those who live and learn in it have on each other—how the environment simultaneously shapes and is shaped by people over time—and the value of each specific context on young children's learning.

Considering Context: Classroom, School, Community

In Chapter 1, the goals of schools were discussed in relation to assessment and the current political climate in the US—are schools places to transmit culture, co-construct culture, or some combination? In a similar vein, environments reflect the goals of schools (often influenced by politics), and embody assessment and accountability in terms of the use of physical space and the materials contained and displayed in those spaces. Expectations for children, and the underlying image of children as held by the teacher, school and broader society, are evident from the moment a person approaches and enters a school. Since children ultimately spend most of their time in their classroom settings, as opposed to the larger school setting, we will begin with a discussion of classroom environments.

Classroom

It is estimated that between kindergarten and third grade, children will spend approximately 4,000 hours in classrooms (Bullard, 2010). For this reason, if no other, adults should heed the words of respected environmental design expert Anita Rui Olds and "design spaces for miracles, not minimums" (2001, p. 13). Recognizing the interplay between environments and the reality of children's experiences living within the classroom walls, the authors of *We are all explorers* (Scheinfeld, Haigh, & Scheinfeld, 2008) suggest five major goals of classroom environments for young children, as illustrated in Figure 2.2. I would suggest a potential physical dimension that is linked to goals of the environment, since benefits of a well-designed classroom environment include brain development. Advances in brain development can be evident in children's ideas and outcomes that are measured in assessments, but can also remain invisible to the naked eye unless communicated through elements in the environment.

Figure 2.2 Five Major Goals of the Classroom Environment

Adapted from Scheinfield, Haigh, and Scheinfeld, 2008.

The extent to which a teacher constructs and adjusts the classroom environment with these interconnected goals in mind is linked with how the environment functions as a constant source of information about young children. This bidirectional flow of information is manifest, for example, in terms of physical space and materials, as well as communication with families and other practitioners. The classroom sends messages about expectations for children's participation and assumptions about children's abilities and appropriate materials:

- Children and families are welcome.
- Beautiful materials and surroundings are valued.
- Children are smart and inventive.
- Flexibility is as important as structure.
- Children's needs are important, and will be met.

Physical Space

Consider the way a physical space affects your mood, your energy, and your interactions with others. The same is true for young children in a classroom context. When young children enter a classroom in the fall, for example, they enter an environment that, while public, takes on an entirely personal meaning and relationship to the child's cognitive and social development. Young people often feel the need to make an impression in their new surroundings to feel ownership and belonging, and teachers who anticipate this desire can help make this a constructive, rather than destructive, process.

A simple and powerful way to enlist the creativity and participation of children and families is to begin the school year with some empty wall space in the classroom. Over time, this wall space can be used to display children's artwork, writing, photos of children and families, and other documentation. The classroom is established from day one as a work in progress, one that evolves based on contributions from all members of the group.

Many teachers are tempted to fill their classrooms with as many bright, colorful, and commercially produced charts, posters, and adornments as they can afford and acquire. There are several reasons why this is not ideal for young children's learning environments. First, a classroom that feels "complete" conveys a feeling that children's contributions to the environment or ideas about design are not necessarily welcome (Felstiner, 2004). "We can make a point of opening up opportunities for children to have influence on the physical space in which they work and play" (p. 41). The systematic welcoming of children's input over their environment resonates with all five of the goals of the environment that were illustrated in Figure 2.2.

I remember the first day of my student teaching experience, when our first grade class gathered together on the rug for our first morning meeting. Ms. Collar addressed the group of children, and made a point of saying that there was a problem in the classroom ("The walls are so BORRRRING!"). She went on in dramatic fashion, bemoaning the fact that the white walls seemed dull and empty, and then suggested that the children might have some ideas about how we could use the space. Over the course of the fall semester the walls grew in synch with the children's learning: alphabet letters painted in colorful acrylic paints snaked their way along the perimeter of the room, self-portraits adorned the reading area, and photos of children and families engaged in classroom activities and field trips were found throughout the room in albums and child-created books. I still admire Ms. Collar's invitation to the children—an invitation to active, not passive learning—and how the process informed us about numerous aspects of the children's development in a completely organic, authentic way.

Materials

While classroom space is one consideration in a classroom environment, materials also impact children's physical and cognitive development and, in turn, inform classroom design. Many American classrooms contain unnecessary clutter that is both distracting and limiting in terms of what it elicits from young children. Countless commercial products (often linked to popular children's television programing), for example, are often brightly colored, plastic, and closed-ended in that children are aware of what they are "supposed" to do with them. Colorful materials may be found in nature, such as leaves, seeds, shells, twigs, pebbles, feathers, and sand. Recycled materials are another source of endless possibilities for learning and inspiration. When these items are collected by children, teachers, and families and displayed in accessible, clear containers, children:

- make connections to nature;
- create unlimited scenarios for exploration and play;
- develop hypotheses about the properties of various objects;
- nurture an appreciation for aesthetics.

When teachers of young children set the stage by thoughtfully "provisioning" the environment (Jones & Nimmo, 1994), simple observation provides educators with a great deal about what connections children are making in the classroom. Table 2.1 provides examples of how noticing (described in detail in Chapter 1) children's use of materials provides information about children's understandings and suggests environmental changes.

Changes to the Setting

Much as noticing children's play and/or behavior provides insights as to how teachers might extend and enhance classroom experiences, so can children's use of space and materials suggest modifications to the classroom environment. A teacher may have a good idea about how children will develop and learn over the course of the year, but will adjust curriculum and supports accordingly to meet the needs of individual students. Similarly, the classroom design can be modified by data that is gathered based on observation and other methods.

Young children in elementary schools, grades K–2, are often introduced to strategies that help them organize their ideas for writer's

Table 2.1 Noticing, Assessment, and Changes to the Environment

Noticing & Questions	Assessment	Changes to Environment
The water table has been used less often than in previous weeks. *Are children tired of playing at the water table? How can I introduce new materials that relate to children's interests?*	Observations of the group's play; photos and/or video of child(ren) at water table; frequency (tallies) or duration (how long) charts.	Change color of water, and/or materials in the water; replace water with another substance; move water table to a new location.
Stephen has a hard time completing his work at the writing table, and seems easily distracted, unable to focus. *Is Stephen's distraction related to the proximity of the dramatic play area? Does Stephen eat breakfast before coming to school?*	Observations of Stephen during center times; photos and/or video of Stephen engaged during writing activities; samples of Stephen's writing; interview with parents; developmental screening/checklist.	Move writing center to different area of room; have basket of snacks available for children if they are hungry during center time.
An argument erupted at lunchtime, about what constitutes a "family." *Do children feel welcome in the classroom? Are the children aware of, respectful of, and tolerant of differences among peers?*	Observations of children during small and large group activity; photos and/or video of children with their family members; family interview or survey; home visit; samples of drawings and/or writing about family themes.	Display images of the children's families; collect and display family artifacts; provide books and toys that represent different family constellations and cultures; invite family "experts" into classroom and document visits in binder that children can explore and expand.

Table 2.2 Sebastian's KWHL Chart About Caterpillars

What I Know	I Want to Know . . .	How I will Learn (collaborators)	I Learned . . .
Caterpillars eat plants.	Do different caterpillars eat different plants?	Observe our class caterpillars. Read a book about caterpillars. Draw in "life cycle" book with friend.	Different caterpillars eat different plants.
Caterpillars' skin is made out of the same thing as fingernails.	Is caterpillar skin hard or soft?	Ask teacher or museum worker. Read a book about caterpillars. Look at websites using computer.	Caterpillar skin is soft.
A caterpillar comes out of a chrysalis, and a moth comes out of a cocoon.	What is a moth before it's a moth?	Read a book about moths. Look at websites using computer. Ask teacher or museum worker. Draw in "life cycle" book with friend.	Moths are also called caterpillars before they change.

workshop and classroom investigations. One example of a tool that teachers use to facilitate children's idea-generation is the KWHL (What I *know*, What I *want* to know, *How* I will find information, and What I *learned*) chart. Systematic use of KWHL charts can serve as a form of assessment that informs teachers of the need for the classroom environment to respond to children's interests and developing skills.

As a result of reading the data contained in Sebastian's KWHL chart, a teacher could:

- borrow books about caterpillars from the school or town library;
- identify computer resources and internet sites related to caterpillars;
- invite a family member or community member with expertise in this area to share some knowledge of caterpillars and/or facilitate hands-on experience with the class.

The notion of the environment as the "third teacher" in the classroom can be seen in this example, where the team is comprised of the classroom teacher, the child, and the environment. The teacher establishes a routine method for outlining and gathering information, the child provides information that serves as self-assessment and data for the teacher to learn about what the child knows, and the environment is adjusted to further inform and support learning. The environment so constructed contributes to the spirit of independence and democracy that is so valued in our educational systems but less often explicitly modeled and assessed. In an educational compact between teacher, child, and environment, there is an interplay and energy that binds the participants in a powerful, lasting way. David Hawkins (1967) referred to an "I-thou-it" relationship between teacher, students, and subject matter. Expanding the "it" to include the classroom environment recognizes how young children "own" and personalize their classroom through shared experience, and co-create a space reminiscent of the cityscape described in the case study in Chapter 1.

School

The bond that exists within a classroom can extend to experiences, assessment, and accountability within a school. The elements of physical space, materials, and adaptability all pertain to the school environment, and send clear messages about expectations, assumptions, and values. "A visitor to any institution for young children tends to size up the messages that the space gives . . . and 'read' its messages or meanings on the basis of personal experience" (Gandini, 1998, p. 162). Personal experiences can include childhood memories, occupation or expertise, as well as influence of the media.

> "Do you call this a school?" She would ask the question in terms more or less politely veiled depending on how far her principles had been outraged. And I could sympathize with her, having served my time in the kind of classroom where each child sits on a bench nailed to the floor, at a desk as firmly fixed in its place, incommunicado as far as all the other children are concerned—and the teacher at the front of the room sternly bound to maintain the discipline without which, it is assumed, the work will not get done.
>
> (Pratt, 1948, p. 3)

The above quote was written almost ten years before the launch of Sputnik in October, 1957—the event often identified as the spark that set off decades of educational pressures and assessment within the US. The progressive environment that Caroline Pratt described in her book (written over 60 years ago) stood in stark contrast to traditional classroom environments that existed at that moment in time. And yet the sentiments expressed in the opening words, "Do you call this a school?" might be overheard today in virtually any public school where a visitor perceives the environment to be less than ideal for a competitive, top world power.

Perception is a powerful thing. I am reminded of my parents telling my brothers and me that the way we dressed and carried ourselves gave an impression (intentional or otherwise) to others, so we should bear that in mind when dressing for a job interview, meeting with a college counselor, and so on. They were trying to discourage us from dyeing our hair magenta and piercing numerous body parts, but their message was clear and simple: there are gatekeepers who hold keys that might be valuable for you and your future, so it's better for you not to give the "wrong" impression. Just as a hiring manager might be put off by the appearance of a job applicant, so too can an educational environment have a negative effect on children, families, and communities.

Figure 2.3 presents examples of signs posted in the entryways of two public schools. The first example, *The Rights of Children*, features the wording posted in the entryway of the Diana School in Reggio Emilia, Italy. The school is one of the municipal preschools in the city, and children aged 3–5 attend the school. The second example is adapted from a poster that greets those who enter a public elementary school in New England. As you compare the two examples side by side, what do you notice? What messages are conveyed about children's competence? How might the messages impact parents and families? Children's motivation?

The Rights of Children	Neighborhood School
Children have the right to have friends, otherwise they do not grow up too well.	Teacher, Parent/Guardian, Student Handbook School Year 2010–2011
Children have the right to live in peace.	
To live in peace means to be well, to live together, to live with things that interest us, to have friends, to think about flying, to dream.	
If a child does not know, she has the right to make mistakes. It works because after she sees the problem and the mistakes she made, then she knows.	**Smart is not something you are; smart is something you GET** **Effort = Success!!** Neighborhood School Principal Asst. Principal
We've got to have rights, or else we'll be sad.	Supervisor of Special Services

Figure 2.3 A Tale of Two Entryways

(Diana School, 1990)

A common criticism of school-wide assessment practices (discussed in detail in Chapter 8) is that the testing feels disconnected to the curriculum that is taught throughout the year. There is also often a lack of communication about both the purpose and results of the testing, and the implications of the results. Teachers and administrators spend a significant portion of the school year in a reactive mode, responding to standards and requirements, and are therefore less present in the moment-to-moment learning that occurs within classrooms and the school.

When the school encourages daily practices such as reflection, collaboration with colleagues and others (e.g. coaches, service providers), and documentation that is visible throughout the school, the school environment shifts. Teachers are both observers and co-learners with children.

> The teachers pick up the children's interests and their ideas, share and discuss them among colleagues, and then return them to the children themselves, engaging them in dialogue and offering tools, materials, and strategies connected with the organization of space to extend those ideas, to combine them, or to transform them ... At the same time the wider system of organization ... sustains teachers, directly and indirectly, in and around the environment of the school, and makes it possible for them to work at this high level of engagement.
>
> (Gandini, 1998, p. 163)

In contrast, Jonathan Kozol (1991) describes classroom, school, and community environments in his acclaimed book, *Savage inequalities*, "where filth and disrepair were worse than anything I'd seen" and wonders "why we would agree to let our children go to school in places where no politician, school board president, or business CEO would dream of working" (p. 5). Amidst the political and economic pressures that currently exist, assessment of young children continues in the hope that enough attention and higher stakes might spur significant change, close the achievement gap, and contribute to our nation's prosperity.

It has been argued that schools, like the communities in which they reside, can be harmful to children and "risky" spaces (Cobb, Danby, & Farrell, 2005). The best-designed assessments in the universe are useless if the children who are being assessed are chronically disadvantaged in terms of their environment, in all of its complexity. The good news is that environments can reflect an image of children as capable and powerful, one layer at a time. This can serve as a powerful intervention in urban, rural, or suburban settings, and in wealthy and poor communities.

Community

Children's relationships with their schools often mirror their connections to the greater environment—the community. Relationships and trust within the community have been shown to correlate with children's and parents' local engagement (Weller & Bruegel, 2009). If part of the responsibility of schools is to prepare future citizens, then research supporting children's development of "spatial autonomy" is relevant. Spatial autonomy refers to freedom associated with spaces, particularly public spaces, according to Weller & Bruegel (2009). Public spaces, such as parks, playgrounds, libraries, and schools invite specific levels of trust and comfort, as well as risk. Concerns about risk in public spaces are typically identified with urban risk. In the assessment arena, risk is associated with fear of making mistakes, which leads to consequences that impact teachers' jobs, schools' funding, and communities' property values. Talk about high stakes!

Parents often adopt strategies they think are "good parenting" to manage children's use of public space, which affects the children's lives in diverse ways. Broader societal concerns about children's competence (e.g. the image of the child) fuel the impression that children need protection from risks and harm.

To borrow language from the economics realm, experts consider "children as passive beneficiaries of their parents' social capital instead of active agents in their own right" (Weller & Bruegel, 2009, p. 631). This is similar to how assessments can lead the public to assume that children are deficient, rather than looking for strengths. As you read the following case study, consider how collaborative efforts led to greater understandings about children's expertise, and bridged classroom and community environments.

Case Study: The Play's the Thing

"She said, 'What are you talking about, doing all this up in Boston? Get down here to Providence!'—that's how it all began," Ben recalled, smiling. Several months ago his long-time friend and colleague had opened the door for a peer network to begin, and look how much they had accomplished in such a short time.

When Ben and Mara first envisioned the peer network they hoped to organize, they discussed bringing together a group of educators from public, private, and non-profit settings in the Boston area. The idea was that meetings would be for learning—people would come to the network armed with documentation from their respective settings, and individuals would share documentation while members of the group asked questions to deepen learning for all involved. The stars had aligned in a perfect way—the NAEYC Professional Development Institute was coming to Providence, Ready to Learn Providence (R2LP) had received a small grant of $10K they could use to fund the project, and Ben had a wild idea about collaborating on a book that would be made available to participants at the Institute. At the very first meeting of the peer network, he tossed out his proposal to the 15 teachers in the room, and despite their already busy work lives they all loved it. It would be called *Places to play in Providence: a guide to the city by our youngest citizens.*

***

"It might be useful if we start with a shared provocation and then at the end we can think about what we've learned from this experience," suggested Ben. The teachers agreed that they would go back to their preschool classrooms and discuss the environment with their students during large group time and in small groups. They were curious to learn what the children actually knew about their own play, but they also had a small concern: What if the children weren't interested in participating? Most of the teachers decided to make this activity a choice for their students, but one classroom teacher decided to make this activity mandatory for her class. She reasoned that since her class was an inclusive preschool classroom, in which many children exhibited developmental delays or other challenges, an attitude of "we're all doing this" was a good strategy.

***

Teachers began collecting drafts of children's stories and drawings to share with the peer network. Ben visited a few classrooms, giving teachers some suggestions about ways to engage children in giving each other feedback about their work. At the peer network's next meeting the group went over the children's work, noticing that several children had added details to their drawings, others had revised their writing, and some had drawn completely new pictures as a result of the feedback process.

With only a few short days before the publishing deadline, a few members of the peer network had a design meeting, using Skype to show each other images that they were talking about. Design experts from Project Zero at the Harvard Graduate School of Education and R2LP coordinated the look and layout of the book, and the final product was ready for production.

***

At a subsequent meeting the teachers shared ways in which this experience had revealed tremendous learning, and they discovered that they had observed some similar behaviors in their respective settings. For instance, some children, who typically never chose to sit and draw, sat and drew (and drew, and drew) pictures about their favorite places to play. Teachers also noticed that children produced more, richer language than usual, especially compared to times past when children had been asked to produce language on demand. The teachers felt they had learned much about the children and their capabilities.

One example that struck Ben in particular occurred when Ben spoke with Marco, age 5, about his drawing. When Marco (bilingual) explained his drawing to Ben (monolingual) in English, his description was recorded as, "Run. Run. Run and jump to the grass. The little kids jump here because they're little. You sit on the benches." When a Spanish-speaking teacher spoke with Marco about his drawing, his description was recorded quite differently:

> Yo corro, yo juego con carros, y también juego con los muchachos. Me gusta jugar juegos con ellos. En el retrato estoy jugando con mis amigos un juego que jugamos cuando yo voy para el parqué: yo corro y busco hojas y juego con las hojas. Yo en el retrato también estaba mirando el sol con mi amigo.
>
> *I run, I play with cars and I also play with my friends. I like to play with them. In the picture I'm playing with my friends a game we play when I go to the park: I run and find leaves and I play with the leaves. In the picture, my friend and I are looking at the sun. In the picture we're looking at the clouds.*

The dramatic difference in the quality of the description reminded the teachers about the importance of authentic assessment that captures children's abilities accurately and responsively.

***

When the first day of the NAEYC Institute arrived, the mayor of Providence, Angel Taveras, took to the stage at the evening event to welcome the thousands of early childhood professionals. A self-proclaimed "Head Start to Harvard kid," he held up a copy of *Places to play in Providence* as he spoke of the efforts of the children and the success of the peer network. Later that morning, as Ben concluded his keynote presentation for a large group of educators, he acknowledged a class of 4-year-olds who had participated in the *Places to play in Providence* collaboration, and whose teacher had brought them to the event to see the impact their work would have on such a large group of people. To their gleeful surprise, they received a standing ovation and jubilant cheers from the crowd.

The learning that occurred as a result of the collaborative efforts of the peer network was shared with thousands of participants at the NAEYC event, and the ripple effects continue as a result of the publication's Internet presence and word of mouth. Ben and Bethany's words sum up some key learning for the children and adults involved in this project:

> Marco learned that combining yellow and red creates orange. Harper learned that a climbing structure at her favorite park has six steps on one side and three on the other for a total of nine. God'iss learned that her friend Shashi could teach her how to make a ladder. Pepper learned that making a good drawing can take a long time. Synai learned that, despite the fact that she had thought it impossible, with persistence and patience she could draw a bicycle. Deeply engaged in this project, children learned literacy skills, the value of writing and drawing, and how to learn with and from others.

> [Adults] learned that children have much to say about where to play in their city. We learned that children with special needs could contribute to this book in authentic ways. We learned that children are capable of giving each other feedback, and that children's support for one another's learning is a habit we want to cultivate.
>
> (R2LP & Project Zero, 2011, p. 19)

Cultural Issues

As the case study demonstrates, classrooms can reflect the children who learn there, and families that live in the surrounding community. Documentation extends the visibility of their ideas and their experiences from the classroom outward, and the use of technology tools makes communication and documentation more accessible than in times past.

Access to information creates challenges from an environmental standpoint, because boundaries need to be established and maintained in innovative ways that keep pace with the levels of communication required of schools and demanded by families. Teachers and administrators sometimes hesitate to invite parents into children's classrooms, presumably because the presence of families affects the power that teachers establish in the classroom.

> Even in conversations about cultural relevance, many of us hold back from sharing the power in our classrooms; we limit ourselves to considerations of things like music, artifacts, and food as ways to bring the lives of families into

the classroom, holding back from asking parents to collaborate with us as we arrange our classroom environments, establish daily rhythms, and make decisions.

(Pelo, 2011, p. 37)

Collaborating with families about environmental considerations certainly entails challenges, but it also opens opportunities for relationships and new perspectives that can promote learning across contexts.

Simple strategies welcome families and community members into the classroom and school environments. As illustrated in Table 2.1, simple noticing can lead to adaptations in the classroom and school environments that send powerful messages to those who enter the space. For example, as one teaching team was considering how best to rearrange their classroom, they decided to include some chairs for adults around the specific areas for work and play. The teachers intentionally sent a message of "welcome" to parents, letting the classroom arrangement convey the teachers' appreciation for observations and interpretation. Parents were asked to contribute their own interpretations and knowledge about children's behavior, which provided multiple perspectives to the teachers' ordinary understandings. Interactions of this sort, among parents and children (their own and other students), allowed families to forge new relationships and strengthen their community (Hilliard, 2011).

Climate: Guidelines and Standards

What guidelines should exist to establish environmental practices and awareness that have a positive impact on children and learning? National accrediting organizations such as NAEYC and the Council on Accreditation (COA) provide guidelines and examples for educators who wish to receive acknowledgment that the school or center is one of high quality. These include recommendations about classroom arrangement and materials, yet these suggestions are merely one piece of a larger need for structure that supports children's well-being. Children's input is not routinely sought when guidelines are developed, as they are typically passive participants, which leaves a notable gap in the design of meaningful assessment.

The lives of children are increasingly governed by adult-designed and enforced regulations. "In the face of risk, adults develop legislation, policies, and practices aimed at protecting children's lives" (Cobb, Danby, & Farrell, 2005, p. 18). The current educational climate suggests that schools are risky places, because the consequences associated with failure affect people's lives in very tangible ways. Current policies and regulations reflect current perspectives of the child in society—children need to be protected (Cobb, Danby, & Farrell, 2005). Lest early childhood classrooms become one more environment that transmits messages about competitiveness and panic to children instead of trust and collaboration, educators must be mindful of the impact of accountability on generations of children in terms of:

- confidence
- perseverance
- conflict resolution
- self-regulation
- creativity
- empathy.

Participants described feelings of intense happiness ("ecstatic memory") in studies of adults' memories of learning environments, when they recalled environmental conditions that were consistently flexible. It sounds like an oxymoron, in that a stable feature of an environment could be its changing and evolving state. The author notes environmental qualities that can combine to provide an individual with a multifaceted sense of environmental freedom. "Freedom was evident as a physical fact and as a state of mind. The environment itself offered freedom in the sense of potentiality—an openness to explorations and discovery in a place that beckoned enthrallingly" (Chawla, 1990, p. 20). Our country was founded on principles anchored in a desire for freedom, and why should public school classrooms communicate anything less?

Children who are free to explore their environments may come upon unexpected discoveries, much like the example of the *flâneur* (wanderer) that Walter Benjamin describes as one "who perfects the art of getting lost within the labyrinth of the city" (1999, p. 9). The very act of wandering opens up possibilities that a scripted path cannot. An environment that promotes exploration and documentation opens up similar possibilities. Such freedom implies trust—trust on the part of teachers that children will learn according to their own interests and abilities; trust on the part of administrators that teachers know best how to teach children according to developmentally appropriate practices; trust on the part of families that schools are places that value their children as individual learners and members of a great citizenry; and trust on the part of children that they will be cared for, respected, and enlisted as active partners in the learning process.

As has been noted in educational research, "high-performing systems generally have a more collaborative and trust-based school culture than typically characterizes the U.S." (Schwartz, Levin, & Gamoran, 2011, p. 34). Drawing inspiration from educators in other countries, we can learn from environments in Reggio Emilia, Italy and design environments for American children that ultimately show how collaborative efforts and ongoing assessment results in "space that reflects their personal lives, the history of their schools, the many layers of culture, and a nexus of well thought-out choices" (Gandini, 1998, p. 177). As you consider various forms of assessment in the chapters that follow, children's interactions with their environment and those in it will continue to emerge as the primary source of information about teaching and learning.

Summary

In this chapter, several features of an early childhood environment that informs, and is informed by, assessment were presented. Although the home environment is typically the one with the most influence on people throughout their lives, children spend thousands of hours in classrooms during their school years, which makes the classroom and school environments critical forces in children's learning. A complex interplay exists between classroom, school, and community environments, and children have an intrinsic need to feel ownership and membership in a public space. Thoughtful design and flexibility provide opportunities for children and families to contribute to documentation and other assessment efforts that evolve over time. The use of space and materials affords possibilities for co-construction of knowledge based on shared experiences. Teachers and parents can use their noticing skills to learn about ways in which the environment is used by children, such as how it can be modified or improved and how it promotes social interaction and/or independence. The current political climate has a direct impact on classroom environments for young children, and the messages that are sent to children about acceptable behaviors (e.g. making mistakes, taking risks) contribute to the level of trust that is manifest in classroom activities and interactions with families.

Now What?

1. What is your reaction to the idea of the environment as the "other" teacher in a classroom? Provide examples of how the environment functions to give feedback about children's abilities and limitations.

2. If the environment is shaped by children, who are likewise shaped by the environment, how does the classroom aesthetic combine with materials to influence a child's identity as a learner?
3. Try to remember an "ecstatic memory" or feelings of intense happiness in a specific setting. Where were you? What are some elements in the setting of that memorable experience that might translate well into an early childhood classroom setting?

Avenues for Inquiry

Places to Play in Providence

This is a publication that resulted from collaboration between early childhood educators and advocates in Providence, RI and education researchers in Cambridge, MA.

http://issuu.com/r2lp/docs/places_to_play_in_pvd

Mayor Angel Taveras's Speech

The speech, at the NAEYC Professional Development Institute, is a nice example of how government leaders can provide support for early childhood professionals.

http://www.youtube.com/watch?v=Ww3QBKzAnKw

Community Playthings

This website is designed to invite exploration of possibilities in urban settings. Drawing inspiration from the Reggio Emilia approach to early childhood education, Karen Haigh discusses principles and practices that transformed settings for children and families. Ongoing collaboration, research, and reflection are discussed.

http://www.communityplaythings.com/resources/articles/Reggio/Reinterpreting.html

3

Observation

Creativity becomes more visible when adults try to be more attentive to the cognitive processes of children than to the results they achieve in various fields of doing and understanding.

(Malaguzzi, 1998, p. 77)

We live in a society that has its eyes focused on the future, and the future can take many forms, such as school outcomes, stock market investments, or global warming. As a society, we don't often take the time to focus on a moment in the moment, particularly in classroom environments, where time is often prescribed and broken into smaller, disconnected blocks. The focus of this chapter is to consider how observation can be used as a tool and a methodology that brings the moment into clearer focus and, in essence, slows down moments of learning so that they can be viewed as invitations to deeper understanding about children's development.

As I was typing the quote from Loris Malaguzzi above, two other quotes flashed through my mind. First, I recalled the familiar idiom often attributed to Machiavelli, "the end justifies the means," which can be interpreted as meaning that the intent behind any action must be considered in the context in which the action was committed to weigh the morality of that specific action. Then, in the millisecond that followed I remembered a passage from Diane Ravitch's book in which she contextualizes her acts in educational policymaking during the George W. Bush presidential era using Scott's (1998) words, "seeing like a state"— viewing schools, teachers, and students "as objects to be moved around by big ideas and great plans" (Ravitch, 2010, p. 10). In Ravitch's interpretation, any policymaker must see "like a state," taking the big-picture perspective, and then in true democratic fashion the pressure is on the policymaker to convince others of the merit of the plans for future success or improvements.

The process of articulating the relationship among these three quotes is an example of what the philosopher Aristotle proposed as the root of inspiration—thinking as a process of moving from one idea to another along a chain of associations. Malaguzzi's words suggest that in focusing solely on the ends (achievement), one misses out on the nuances in children's cognitive processes. Machiavelli's words suggest that focus on the ends, or outcomes, is necessary to achieve a desired goal, and Ravitch's explanation of "seeing like a state" suggests that the ends-first focus is a necessary cog in the democratic wheel. Systematic observations of children provide associations and insight that contribute to creative outputs, focus on process, and support democratic practice. Observation and documentation provide method and means, and greater under- standing for children (and potentially all citizens) is the end result. For a society focused on the future, taking time to examine the present is a worthwhile investment.

The challenge for American educators and policymakers is to reframe understanding about the goals and benefits of assessment. Teachers make decisions daily that impact classroom environment, rules, and expectations for children's development. As is the case with any set of expectations, there is a risk that in the process of looking to meet our goals, we are inclined to see what we want to see and miss or ignore what we don't want to see. Engaging in an assessment process with observation (supported with documentation) at the core, allows us to evaluate young children's learning more objectively and enlist others in a collaborative, public cycle that incorporates goal setting and reflection. Figure 3.1 illustrates this assessment cycle. Because public education is a public investment, national standards exist to encourage educators to maximize the benefits of their teaching practice and assessment cycle.

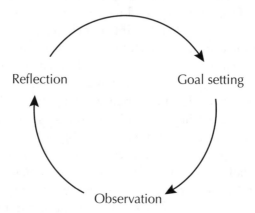

Figure 3.1 Assessment Cycle

Setting Goals

From an economic perspective, observation skills bring in big returns on investment if teachers and practitioners use their skills in focused and accomplished ways. As teachers and schools are being held increasingly accountable for the learning that occurs in their classrooms, it is in the best interest of teachers and schools to promote observation practices that inform teachers about their students' progress as well as their own professional and personal growth. National, state, and local standards offer or require the goals that a teacher sets for students in her classroom, whereby teachers' knowledge of child development and individual differences is confirmed through observation. This, in turn, validates and informs teaching decisions on many levels, from the most intimate level (classroom) to the legislative (policy) level.

Two examples of standards that have had a ripple effect on classroom practice and teacher preparation are the National Board for Professional Teaching Standards (NBPTS) propositions for effective teaching (2001) and the Model Core Teaching Standards (2010) drafted by the Council of Chief State School Officers (CCSSO). Figure 3.2 illustrates the five propositions that NBPTS developed in an attempt to capture the essence of effective teaching, specifically that teachers interact with children and peers as opposed to simply transmitting information to passive students, which research evidence had denoted as less effective practice (Borich,

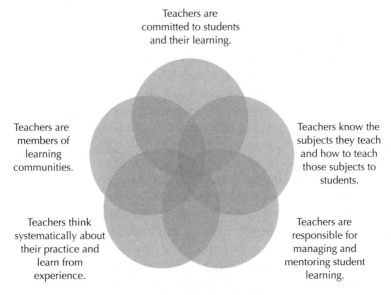

Figure 3.2 NBPTS Propositions for Effective Teaching

2011). You will notice language woven throughout the propositions that is in synch with the notion of collaborative assessment as presented throughout this book. For example, "learning communities" resonates with the learning group discussed in Chapter 1, as does the idea that teachers are "responsible" for and "committed" to their students' learning.

Similarly, the standards listed in Table 3.1 have been proposed to apply to all professional educators. Originally, the standards were designed to ensure that new teachers would uphold certain standards of practice, but since teaching and learning are lifetime endeavors, the benefits of high quality, effective teaching cannot be underemphasized. The standards contain language consonant with a developmentally appropriate perspective on teaching and learning, diversity, inquiry, and collaboration. Woven together, the language of such educational standards provides a sturdy support net for reflective practice that places observation at the core.

Looking *and* Listening

Many people assume that observation entails merely watching children, and perhaps taking notes. Indeed, the pace of many classroom settings has made the use of Post-it® notes a common practice, as teachers scribble notes on the paper throughout the day, and then stick those small papers into children's folders, to be revisited later. While not a frivolous practice, such sporadic note taking does not capture or present a full picture of a child engaged in a specific activity. Unless a teacher incorporates systematic observation into the daily classroom routine, observation records will likely be inconsistent. This can lead to mis-interpretation of children's behavior and, ultimately, misleading information that is detrimental to a child's image to self and others.

One way to approach observation is to consider it as a multisensory process. A teacher takes in information using many senses, but primarily looking and listening. Italian educator Carlina Rinaldi has written extensively and presented around the world, promoting ideas about what she calls "the pedagogy of listening" (Rinaldi, 2006, p. 65). Rinaldi has defined listening with a scholar's eye (and ear) for detail—masterfully weaving the art, science, psychology, sociology, and philosophy strands associated with listening into practical provocations for teachers and schools. Table 3.2 contains the core of Rinaldi's definition of listening, which serves as an invitation to dialogue about how this might influence classroom practices. When teachers and children listen to each other and to themselves, the teaching and learning relationship shifts. The culture of learning in the classroom changes, from one in which the teacher notices the learning that

Table 3.1 Model Core Teaching Standards

Standard 1: Learner Development
The teacher understands how children learn and develop, recognizing that patterns of learning and development vary individually within and across the cognitive, linguistic, social, emotional, and physical areas, and designs and implements developmentally appropriate and challenging learning experiences.

Standard 2: Learning Differences
The teacher uses understanding of individual differences and diverse communities to ensure inclusive learning environments that allow each learner to reach his/her full potential.

Standard 3: Learning Environments
The teacher works with learners to create environments that support individual and collaborative learning, encouraging positive social interaction, active engagement in learning, and self-motivation.

Standard 4: Content Knowledge
The teacher understands the central concepts, tools of inquiry, and structures of the discipline(s) he or she teaches and creates learning experiences that make these aspects of the discipline accessible and meaningful for learners.

Standard 5: Innovative Applications of Content
The teacher understands how to connect concepts and use differing perspectives to engage learners in critical/creative thinking and collaborative problem solving related to authentic local and global issues.

Standard 6: Assessment
The teacher understands and uses multiple methods of assessment to engage learners in their own growth, to document learner progress, and to inform the teacher's ongoing planning and instruction.

Standard 7: Planning for Instruction
The teacher draws upon knowledge of content areas, cross-disciplinary skills, learners, the community, and pedagogy to plan instruction that supports every student in meeting rigorous learning goals.

Standard 8: Instructional Strategies
The teacher understands and uses a variety of instructional strategies to encourage learners to develop deep understanding of content areas and their connections, and to build skills to access and appropriately apply information.

Standard 9: Reflection and Continuous Growth
The teacher is a reflective practitioner who uses evidence to continually evaluate his/her practice, particularly the effects of his/her choices and actions on others (students, families, and other professionals in the learning community), and adapts practice to meet the needs of each learner.

Standard 10: Collaboration
The teacher collaborates with students, families, colleagues, other professionals, and community members to share responsibility for student growth and development, learning, and well-being.

Source: Council of Chief State School Officers (2010).

Table 3.2 Definitions of Listening

Listening as sensitivity to patterns that connect and connect us to others.

Listening as a metaphor for openness and sensitivity to listen and be listened to with all of our senses.

Listening to the hundred, the thousand languages, symbols, and codes we use to express ourselves.

Listening as time, the time of listening, a time that is outside chronological time.

Listening is emotion; it is generated by emotions and stimulates emotions.

Listening as welcoming and being open to differences.

Listening as an active verb that involves interpretation, giving meaning to the message and value to those who offer it.

Listening that does not produce answers but formulates questions.

Listening is not easy. It requires a deep awareness and at the same time a suspension of our judgments and above all our prejudices.

Listening that takes the individual out of anonymity.

Listening as the premise for any learning relationship.

Listening, therefore, as "a listening context," where one learns to listen and narrate, where individuals feel legitimated to represent their theories and offer their own interpretations of a particular question.

Adapted from: Rinaldi (2001:80–81).

takes place to one in which learning is created *and* noticed by all members of the group, thereby raising levels of understanding as a result of the observation process (Fiore & Rosenquest, 2010).

Recording Observations

Teachers want to be effective practitioners, capturing rich data about children's abilities and responding to mandates set by education standards. A solid strategy for gathering data is useful for many reasons, and forces teachers to ask themselves questions such as:

- What is a realistic amount of time that I will be able to set aside to observe children each day?
- How can I prepare the classroom so that I may observe and the children are engaged in self-sustaining activity if needed?
- How will I analyze and report my observation data?
- With whom will I share my thoughts and seek expert opinion?

- What is the best method of recording information?
- How will I know if formal testing is warranted?

Different approaches to observing children require different amounts of time and materials. The more time needed, the more a teacher must rely on a co-teacher or assistant to help with classroom activity while she observes.

If a teacher chooses to use technology, such as a digital audio recorder or video recorder, those devices can be set up in the classroom and left to function while the teacher goes about the daily routine, and then later the teacher can listen to or watch the recordings and see what she was unable to see during the "live" action earlier in the day. One huge benefit of recording children's activity is that digital audio and video afford the convenience of revisiting interesting moments by simply rewinding and playing over and over again.

When any observer tries to capture a full, accurate picture of a child, it is impossible to capture every single detail of any given situation. Whether it is because a teacher is looking down at her paper while jotting down notes, or because a video camera is angled a certain way and therefore misses one corner of the classroom, it is crucial to note that no one observation is perfect. Likewise, no one observation on any given day can represent a child's full range of abilities. Every child has "off" days, as does every teacher, so a rule of any assessment strategy is that a child must be observed multiple times in order to gain a sense of confidence in what is being represented. Taking this one step further, a child should be recorded using multiple methods of observations. Several methods are described below, and are commonly used by early childhood practitioners in order to gain and revisit information that lends itself to greater insights into young children's learning.

Anecdotal Notes

Anecdotal notes are best suited for the "Post-it®" method of observing young children. These are brief notes taken to capture a specific incident that occurs during the course of a day or designated activity. The teacher records what happened and some contextual details to help her remember the scene for future reference. An example of this would be Sam speaking in the dramatic play area about the new baby he has in his tummy. He says, "Mommy has a baby in her tummy—it's my new brother! I have a baby in my tummy—her name is Clara." In this case, the teacher might jot down Sam's words and play, including his playmates. She may then make a note to bring books about siblings into the book area and plan to have "baby bath time" as a choice in the water table soon.

Running Records

These notes can be taken on an individual or a small group of children. The idea is that the teacher begins writing at the start of the observation period and doesn't stop until the end of the allotted time. The teacher records everything the child says and does, including as much detail as possible for future revisiting. For example, the teacher is watching Talia and Brendyn interact with "Steve the Science Guy," who has come to visit their first grade class and talk about weather. The teacher begins by writing some notes about context (e.g. time of day, location, number of children) and drawing a sketch of what the table looks like in terms of materials (e.g. wide plastic straw, small marble, rectangular cardboard box) and seating arrangements. Once she begins writing, she tries to include snippets of dialogue and vivid details such as tone of voice and body language.

Later, as she types up the running record from her notes, she makes sure to include information about the following, if possible:

- How did each child react to and respond to the other?
- How was behavior initiated?
- How was behavior subdued?
- What were reactions of peers to the behavior?
- What were reactions of adults to the behavior?

It is important that notes are typed in the order that events occurred, so to be true to the actual time period that is observed. For example, when one child is observed acting aggressively toward another child, it is quite relevant if the first child lashed out unprovoked, or if she was hit in the head by the other child, prompting retaliation.

Teachers often devise short cuts, such as abbreviations and symbols that help to make the recording process less cumbersome and more streamlined. The polished running record will be placed in the children's files, along with other running records obtained over the course of the year. These running records provide useful information about a child's development over time. Such "snapshots" are useful when discussing a child's progress with parents, administrators, or specialists, but they are also useful along the way, as information is gathered. Observational data in running records helps answer questions that arise about a child's behavior, friendships, and interests. The data validates hunches or hypotheses that develop, and also inform curriculum planning that can build upon children's interests.

Student Notebooks

Some teachers incorporate running records into notebooks or daily logs that are kept for each child. During free play or outside time, a teacher can often find a quiet spot to sit for a few minutes and observe, while writing into the child's individual notebook. To use this method most efficiently, some teachers select a few children to observe each day, keeping track of which children are to be observed on a given day and noting holidays or field trips that might interrupt a scheduled observation day. Or, a teacher and co-teacher or assistant may divide up the class and gather brief observation notes about all of the children everyday into daily logs. Daily notes can be synthesized into some "big ideas" or "take-aways" for that week that are also included in the notebooks. Clearly, this method of recording observations is time-consuming, but families very much appreciate the feedback.

Another cautionary note relating to running records and other forms of written notes is that these notes are taken as the events are filtered through the lens of one individual. As previously mentioned, while a teacher is busily writing, she may miss some action that therefore does not get included in the notes. Also, because human beings are prone to biases and interpretations based on our own experiences, it sometimes happens that our notes reflect some of these biases. A useful strategy to minimize the presence and impact of bias is observing with a colleague from time to time. Two sets of eyes often notice different things, and the result of consolidating two sets of notes into one means that teachers will need to discuss and negotiate interpretations in order to report the most accurate account of events. *Inter-rater reliability* is the term used to refer to how closely aligned two raters' ratings are, and this will be discussed in greater detail in the next chapter. For the purposes of this discussion, it is important to note that a high inter-rater reliability, such as 98 percent, means that two different people are seeing and interpreting in quite similar ways. That number is significant from the standpoint of scientific research, which often regards numerical (quantitative) data as more objective, and therefore more important.

Checklists

A quicker way to gather observational data, and one that is typically easy to convert into numerical data, is the use of checklists. There are checklists that accompany commercial curricula, as well as checklists that teachers create themselves in order to answer questions relating to a specific goal. Examples of checklists include:

- Frequency—tally marks are used to note how many times specific behaviors occur or skills are observed. For instance, how often does Brian interrupt Ms. Iskric during circle time? How often does Matthew complete his math tasks successfully at the math center?
- Duration—tally marks are used to represent five-minute intervals. For example, how much of Hiroki's choice time is spent with him displaying unfocused, uninvolved behavior? How much time does it take Calliope to enter into play with peers at recess?

As with other forms of observational assessment, caution is needed here in terms of the value with which people imbue checklists. Checklists are most effective when the data gathered fits well with the philosophy of the classroom and school, and the instrument does not lead to mis-interpretation of children's abilities and motivation. A preschool teacher at a charter school, Ms. M., once spoke to me of her concern that the school's director was using the MA state *Guidelines for preschool learning experiences* (2003) as an assessment tool, rather than for curriculum planning. Despite the document's clear statement that "[g]uidelines focus on what staff should do to help young children develop needed skills and knowledge rather than on what children are expected to know and do at the age of three and four" (p. 3), the experiences were being used as a checklist that teachers were told to use to evaluate children's abilities.

The teacher explained how, in one instance, a guideline under the Life Sciences section, which is linked to a Preschool Curriculum standard under "States of Matter," was being utilized as a checklist. Teachers were asked to check off the individual items below as discrete skills for each child, instead of using the items as examples of experiences that would help children develop the suggested skills laid out in the guideline:

> Explore, describe, and compare the properties of liquids and solids found in children's daily environment.
> - Manipulate and describe materials such as water, sand, clay, play dough.
> - Explore ways materials can be changed by freezing/melting; dissolving (e.g. sugar crystals or gelatin in water); combining materials (e.g. earth + water

= mud); physical force (e.g. pushing, pulling, pounding, stretching materials such as play dough or clay).

- Experiment with "magic mixtures" of common materials (e.g. flour, baking soda, cornstarch, water, salt, vinegar, food color), observe the results, then describe their experiments to others.

(p. 24)

The concern that Ms. M. shared is important because it echoes a position shared by many in the early childhood field—as more time is required to teach children specific skills, less time is available for close observation of children. The benefits of observation, including the opportunity to collaborate with children and peers, cannot be achieved with unidirectional measures.

Developmentally appropriate experiences are being replaced with higher expectations and benchmarks that are simply not in line with young children's cognitive and physical development. Using the example above, even if a kindergarten student was able to articulate what happens when vinegar is added to a baking soda mixture, he may be incapable of executing the fine motor skills needed to carry out the experiment. Anecdotal notes or a running record for this child would provide insights into his cognitive and physical development. This means that the more time a child is observed exploring, playing, and developing self-confidence through experiences like the science experience above, the more true classroom practice is to the intention for which the experiences were designed—with a potential byproduct being the foundation for a child's lifetime love of learning.

Reflective Practice

A love of learning is a key component of the disposition that many teachers of young children possess. It was described by Dewey (1910/1933) as an attitude or way of thinking that welcomes inquiry and uncertainty, similar to the notion of inquiry as stance proposed by Cochran-Smith & Lytle (2009). When teachers engage in reflective practice, they use observation to notice children's learning in the moment, revisit moments of learning through the use of documentation, and plan for future classroom activity. In this sense, teaching practice is constantly evolving in the same manner that children's learning evolves, and children and teachers become partners in the learning process. Several examples of reflective practice are described below, and the examples represent different levels of reflection. Early childhood practitioners engage in each level of reflection, alone and with others, in order to gain insights into their teaching and young children's learning.

Shallow Reflection

When teachers and practitioners engage in shallow reflection, they are often noticing progress with respect to certain goals. This is often the type of reflection that gets shared with families in the form of newsletter and bulletin boards posted inside and outside the classroom space. For example, a teacher might observe how many letters her preschoolers are able to recognize, and then reflect on how she might keep students focused on the alphabet in small group activities. A second grade teacher might notice that children were fidgety during a large group discussion about the town library, and then reflect on ways to help students pay attention during large group discussions.

Applied Reflection

When teachers are able to make connections between theory and practice, they are able to make connections between their observations, educational theory, and new applications. These syntheses are manifest in the classroom through the use of KWHL charts, for example, as a first grade teacher uses them to see what children know, want to know, and how they will go about learning something new. Through the use of these charts, the first grade teacher can observe children's learning, and reflect upon her own efficacy in the classroom in helping students connect new understanding to previous knowledge. A preschool teacher might notice her 3-year-olds getting cranky while waiting for her to pass out snacks, and reflect upon ways to provide opportunities for children to develop autonomy in the classroom.

Analytical Reflection

This type of reflection expands teachers' observations and reflections to consider issues outside of their classroom walls. Teachers engaged in analytical reflection recognize that their actions have consequences, and that classroom practices are linked to larger social, political, and ethical issues. A preschool teacher might observe that some children get more turns at being line leader than others, even though they use an "eeny, meeny, miny, mo" song to choose who will lead their line each day. The teacher might engage the class in activity to find an equitable, democratic practice for selecting a daily line leader, and reflect upon ways that every child has opportunities to demonstrate leadership in the classroom. A second grade teacher who observes students in leveled reading groups might reflect upon whether differentiated instruction within groups would provide non-native English speaking students with more opportunities for success in the classroom. She might further reflect on ways to document students' successes in the classroom, and invite parent volunteers in to help take photos and record dialogue.

Self-reflection

Putting it all together—a teacher uses the observations she's collected and her awareness of the greater landscape for education to consider her own teaching practice. Student teaching seminars often use journals as a way for students to begin the systematic process of writing about classroom experiences, explicitly asking students to record specific moments and look for ways that their individual biases, beliefs, and values impact classroom practices. Such reflective practices are valuable to novice teachers as well as seasoned veterans. Many of Vivian Paley's books, such as *The girl with the brown crayon* (1998), provide excellent examples of reflective practice, and feature specific moments of self-reflection.

Observation and reflection provide teachers and children with short- and long-term benefits. As a result of close observation, teachers may develop empathy that was not felt before, with respect to a specific child or group of children. Empathy is as important for young children as it is for teachers, so modeling behaviors through the use of documentation helps create a classroom environment that is respectful to all members of the group. The act of collaborating with colleagues, parents and families, and inviting children to be primary, active participants in their learning experiences establishes strong relationships that shape highly engaging classroom experiences that reverberate throughout the school, home environments, and broader community. A key component of observing young children is the recording of the observations. It is therefore critical to examine the means by which observation becomes visible, and shared by more than one individual, in a democratic classroom environment.

Documentation as Noun (Product) and Verb (Process)

Documentation is more than words on a piece of paper, more than a simple photograph, and more than "window dressing" or pretty bulletin board displays. Documentation "is not just a teaching tool, but a pedagogical philosophy of knowing and valuing children" (Turner & Wilson, 2010, p. 5). Many educators, looking for ways to capture children's learning and convey children's competence, have embraced strategies that have observation at the core, and then include evaluative elements. Some examples are portfolios and work-sampling strategies.

What distinguishes documentation as it is considered in this book is its relationship to products and process. So often assessment is focused on an end goal or product, without recognizing the process as valuable. Educators who systematically document children's and teachers' thinking often compare the process to that of detectives, anthropologists, or, more aptly, archeologists who "seek to position the subject or object in a time, a place, a culture" (p. 6). The educators may differ in their approaches to observing and documenting children's learning, but the attitude they possess is similar, and features an underlying desire to learn something that will shift the culture of the classroom environment and strengthen their teaching.

Carlina Rinaldi has specifically noted the teaching-learning relationship and how it is impacted by the use of documentation:

> At the moment of documentation (observation and interpretation), the element of assessment enters the picture immediately, that is, in the context and during the time in which the experience (activity) takes place. It is not sufficient to make an abstract prediction that establishes what is significant—the elements of value necessary for learning to be achieved—before the documentation is actually carried out. It is necessary to interact with the action itself, with that which is revealed, defined, and perceived as truly significant, as the experience unfolds.
>
> (2001, p. 85)

Documentation provides insights into teaching practices, as a result of recording, analyzing, and sharing observations of young children. During this process, teachers and children are engaged in active, ongoing reflection that is supported by artifacts (photos, video clips, samples of students' work and conversation), and inspires further inquiry and action.

Turning Observation into Advocacy

The act of creating and sharing documentation with young children is extremely valuable and empowering. Children see their faces, words, and work as keys to opening new knowledge doorways. Teachers can help families and administrators understand the meaning that the learning group has created as a result of their work, and can connect the learning to federal, state, and local standards. Throughout this process, and by virtue of the products gathered and created, children "discover that they 'exist' and can emerge from anonymity and invisibility, seeing that what they say and do is important, is listened to, and is appreciated: it is a value" (Rinaldi, 2001, p. 87). The case study below provides an example of how collaboration and documentation made visible the value of one child in an elementary school setting.

Case Study: Communicating Competence

Lori, a Speech and Language Pathologist at Ocean Elementary School, and Elena, a Special Education professor at a college in California, have been collaborating for over ten years with the school faculty and interns to observe and assess children. Their work focuses on gathering documentation that captures development and progress over time, and provides a contrast to testing that captures children's learning based on a brief period of time, or a single numerical test score. Recently, their focus has turned to documentation of children whose progress seems slow, and whose subtle advances can easily go unnoticed and undervalued.

One of their favorite experiences involves a little girl in second grade, Lakshanya. Lori and Elena had been observing Lakshanya for two years, starting when Lakshanya and her family moved to California from India and Lakshanya was 5 years old. When she arrived at the Ocean School, and for the first two years of her public school experience, Lakshanya did not initiate verbal speech, showed very little affect, and was socially isolated from her peers. One assessment deemed her mentally retarded. She depended on adults in the classroom to anticipate and respond to her needs. Although her parents repeatedly claimed that she spoke freely with them at home, in their native Hindi, they admitted that English was not a language any of them felt confident speaking.

***

Lori decided to try and create an environment for Lakshanya where she could observe peers modeling gestures and language. She chose two girls from Lakshanya's class—Claudia and Grace—to accompany Lakshanya to one of her speech therapy sessions. The girls were selected because of their friendly, verbal dispositions, and Lori decided to let their own interests and questions spark interactions between the girls, since Lakshanya rarely initiated interactions of any kind. Right away, Claudia noticed the different shoes that each girl was wearing, and asked, "Do our shoes make us a different height?" This prompted a comparison of the girls' heights, and comparisons with and without shoes. Claudia modeled a way to compare heights using her gaze and a hand gesture. When it was Lakshanya's turn to compare her peers' heights, she used her own hand gesture, moving the hair on Claudia's head to compare Claudia's height with Grace's height. As Lori took photos throughout this session, she realized that this documentation was important because it showed Lakshanya initiating a non-verbal turn, following Claudia's model.

***

Excited by this development, Elena suggested that she and Lori structure a small group activity. They organized a group of six children—three with language or social needs and three classmates. The activity involved the children watching a video of children dancing to music and playing the "Freeze" game, and then they played a brief Freeze game themselves. After their game, Lori and Elena invited the children to draw a group picture (on a large piece of paper) of them (the children) dancing and freezing in their poses. Elena recorded this session on her video camera, and noticed that Lakshanya was the last child to bring her pencil to the paper. The children first drew their own images, and then three of the children began noticing the others' drawings and talking about them, which prompted the addition of imaginary animals and a robot. Rather than joining the children's discussion and negotiations, Lakshanya engaged in parallel drawing, and did not connect her figures to the drawings of other children.

The following week, Lori and Elena had a scheduled session with Lakshanya. Lori and Elena decided in advance that they would show her the video Elena had taken the previous week during the group session—dancing and drawing the "Freeze." As Elena began videotaping the session, and Lori began preparing the videotape of the small group in the VCR, Lakshanya began spontaneously naming the children in the small group. This was the first time she had initiated a conversation, or had contributed language other than "yes" or "no." Wanting to extend this exciting new development, Elena stopped recording and showed Lakshanya some of the video she had just taken of Lakshanya speaking with Lori.

Lori reconvened the small group of six children to show them the videotape of their previous "Freeze" session. While other children leaned on or against the round table, Lakshanya sat back in her seat, apart from the group, and responded with one-word answers when prompted by Lori. Lori invited the rest of the group to ask Lakshanya a question and help her to be part of the conversation. One classmate, Nathan, offered support, asking, "What do you think—work by ourselves or in a group?" Lakshanya responded, "Group."

***

Lori and Elena continue to document Lakshanya's spontaneous interactions with her peers and teachers, in the classroom and in small groups during recess, snack time, and lunch. They now record her participation in music therapy sessions, and have visited her family's home to share their documentation. Because of the photos and video footage they have collected, they can inform Lakshanya's parents and school staff of ways to facilitate verbal communication. Whereas she was once considered incapable of functioning at grade level due to mental deficiencies, Lakshanya now participates with support of district specialists, including an occupational therapist, and an assistive technology therapist who provides software options for both the home and school environment.

The historical perspective afforded by documentation (photos, video clips, samples of Lakshanya's work) has made her progress visible over time. Lori is able to show the evolution of communication: grunts, eye contact, single-word responses, and higher levels of communication.

The case study above is reminiscent of the classic philosophical question, "If a tree falls in the woods and no one is there to hear it, does it make a sound?" We could ask a similar question, "If a child says something intelligent but no one is there to document it, is a child competent?" Both questions are about observation and reality, and about a philosophical stance toward children and education. It is clear that teaching and assessment involve looking *and* listening, documentation *and* advocacy. Observation is one means of perceiving children's competence, and in the chapters that follow alternative means of establishing children's competence will be presented for your consideration. First, you will need to stop thinking about the tree.

Summary

Throughout this chapter, an emphasis on observation that incorporates reflection and documentation of young children was presented. Approaching the study of young children through a lens that welcomes co-construction of meaning is quite different than a lens that is already focused on what it expects to see. While standards and guidelines are helpful for identifying common values in early childhood classrooms, there is value in holding the big educational picture as well as noticing the little learning moments as they naturally occur in the classroom. There is growing recognition that teachers and children want to slow down the pace of classroom activity, and a cycle of goal setting, observation, and reflection helps achieve this goal. Observation is a multi-sensory experience, and documentation also takes many forms, such as photographs, video clips, samples of students' work, and excerpts from children's and/or adults' conversations. Teachers, interns, parent volunteers, and others are welcome contributors to the documentation process, and the act of publicly sharing artifacts of children's learning shifts the educational culture away from a strict transmission model to one that acknowledges and values process as crucial to meaning-making, and children as competent, active learners.

Now What?

1. The various methods of recording observations give people chances to capture data that is otherwise ignored or invisible in most standardized assessments. How might you argue the value of scheduling required observation periods into every school day?
2. Why is the systematic use of documentation so important in early childhood education? Describe one example of something you have read or seen in the media that supports the use of documentation products or process.
3. What are some ethical considerations regarding the use of documentation? What policies could be developed to maximize the benefits of family participation with observation and documentation?

Avenues for Inquiry

Council of Chief State School Officers (CCSSO)

This website provides resources related to the INTASC standards. Publications, programs, and digital resources relate to what all teachers should know and be able to do across educational contexts.

http://www.ccsso.org/resources/programs/interstate_teacher_assessment_consortium_(intasc).html videatives.com

This website provides archives of video clips of young children and analytical narratives (video + narrative = videative) that are indexed by various categories, including age and topic of interest. The videos, taken in real classrooms by real teachers, afford viewers the opportunity to observe children in ordinary classroom activities and to revisit precise moments to enhance learning and generate dialogue about what is noticeable.

http://www.videatives.com

Boulder Journey School's virtual tour

This link takes you to the Virtual Tour webpage for the Boulder Journey School, in Boulder, CO. As you look at the slideshow, you are able to see how documentation is used and displayed throughout the school and in the individual classrooms. You will also be able to see quotes from children, families, and visitors that speak to the relationship that exists between the school and others.

http://www.boulderjourneyschool.com/Pages/Home/Virtual_Tour.htm

4

Standardized Assessment

> Don't let anyone tell you that standardized tests are not accurate measures. The truth of the matter is they offer a remarkably precise method for gauging the size of the houses near the school where the test was administered.
>
> (Kohn, 2001)

The tone of the above quote captures some of the frustration educators, particularly early childhood educators, have felt over many years. Taking a humorous stab at the grim realities that have resulted over decades of increased testing and evaluation, Alfie Kohn addresses many issues relating to education, among other topics, in his writing. As a result of following scientific and statistical evidence comparing high scores on standardized tests and levels of learning, Kohn argues that "as a rule, better standardized exam results are more likely to go hand-in-hand with a shallow approach to learning than with deep understanding" (Kohn, 2001, p. 348). As an advocate for children and teachers, Kohn posits that those "who work most closely with kids are the most likely to understand how harmful standardized testing is. Many teachers—particularly those who are very talented—have what might be described as a dislike/hate relationship with these exams" (p. 349).

It is important to remember that standardized assessment is a broader construct than standardized testing, which has been the focus of so much concern in educational dialogue. The underlying purpose of standard practices of any kind is consistency, so that results can be compared. Standardized assessment in early childhood classrooms takes many forms, ranging from checklists that teachers fill out to cutting tasks that children complete. Standardized assessment can also refer to elaborately structured assessments in which "procedures and instruments are specified, teachers are trained in how to use them, and the assessments are expected to be consistent" across settings (McAfee, Leong, & Bodrova, 2004, p. 57). Yet because standardized tests, specifically, are especially controversial in early childhood, a good deal of attention will be paid to standardized testing. In order to advocate intelligently for developmentally appropriate practices, understanding the many facets of the standardized testing context is critical.

Children's perspectives on standardized testing are important to consider, as testing has become a significant part of the public school culture. Several children's book authors have written about the testing situation in an attempt to quell the anxiety that exists for children, families, teachers, and administrators. For example, *Testing Miss Malarkey* (Finchler, 2000) describes the impact that a standardized test, the I.P.T.U. test, has on the school culture. At recess the children play Multiplication Mambo, the cafeteria lady serves "good brain food," and the gym teacher insists they prepare mentally and physically with meditation and "something called 'yogurt.'"

In a similar vein, the popular children's book series featuring Junie B. Jones has a special book titled *Junie B.'s essential survival guide to school* (Park, 2009). In this comprehensive book, Junie shares her opinions about many school topics, including tests. Table 4.1 lists some of Junie's

Table 4.1 Junie B. Jones's Wisdom About Tests

TESTS is the school word for when teachers teach you stuff. Only *they don't believe* that you actually learned anything. So they *pass out questions for you to answer* so you can *prove* you remembered something.

TESTS ARE NOT FUN.

When a test is getting passed out, children feel PRESSURE in their heads.
Also, their hands get wettish.
And their throats can't swallow that good.

That is how you feel for the whole entire time the test is on your desk by the way.
Then finally you finish.
And you hand it in.
And your teacher takes it home and puts a grade on it.

GRADE is the school word for TEST LETTER.
I do not know why they don't just call it TEST LETTER. But that is not the way their minds work.

A+ is the biggest grade that you can get.
That kind of grade makes parents smile as big as they can.

B+ makes them smile, too.
But they don't show their teeth as much.

If you get a C they just look at you.

With a D or F they suck their cheeks way into their heads.
You do not even want to *see* what *this* face looks like.

Adapted from Park (2009).

thoughtful opinions of tests. As humorous as these examples are, the anxiety and impact on children's self-esteem are quite real. Yet it's important not to confuse testing with assessment before jumping on the "tests are evil" bandwagon.

It is interesting to note that the word "assessment" evolved from the Latin word "assidere," which combines "sedere" (sit) and "ad" (beside). Indeed, children seem to spend much classroom time sitting for assessments, but not often with teachers next to them to support and scaffold their work. Much of the confusion is due to the words "assessment," "measurement," and "evaluation" being used as synonyms. It would be more accurate to distinguish moments of child-teacher collaboration as examples of assessment, where a teacher truly extends and enhances learning opportunities for children as they work toward greater understanding and mastery of concepts.

Recognizing that assessment takes many forms, the National Association for the Education of Young Children (NAEYC) articulated four reasons for assessment of young children: 1) to support teaching and learning; 2) to recognize children in need of intervention or support services; 3) to evaluate early childhood programs and monitor trends; and 4) for high-stakes accountability (2003, p. 10). The authors caution against making any decisions that can potentially harm children's future educational opportunities, acknowledging the real concern about a mismatch between assessment tools and design and the capabilities of young children being assessed. Beginning with a teacher's desire to make an informed and intelligent decision, appropriate assessment tools can be selected to provide accurate information about children's learning, which can then inform teaching practices. In this chapter we will explore the ways standardized assessment has been used in an effort to minimize bias, increase reliability, and generalize information.

Traditional Assessment

Traditional assessment generally means tests. Traditional tests are often contrasted with authentic assessments, which are the focus of Chapter 5. Whereas authentic assessments are considered directly linked to children's knowledge and performance in a particular learning context, traditional tests are assumed to capture and represent knowledge out of context, in a standardized format that can be replicated and produce predictable results.

Looking to language to shed some light on how traditional assessment has become equated with tests, the origin of the word "test" is noteworthy—the Latin "testum," meaning "earthen pot." This evolved into an early definition (small vessel used to analyze precious metals), which is fairly consistent with its present-day connotation of establishing the worth or value of something. For young children, traditional assessment conjures up images of pencil and paper tasks. In fact, a quick computer search of "test" using Google images yields a host of images, including:

- hand-held pencils poised above fill-in-the-bubble multiple choice answer boxes;
- cartoon children with sweat droplets spritzing—radiating—into the air around their heads;
- nuclear bomb mushroom clouds.

So how did a small earthen vessel come to evoke mushroom cloud devastation? We are situated at a particular moment in time when many educators and families have come to the conclusion that traditional assessments are damaging children in many ways. The Latin phrase, "primum non nocere" means "first, do no harm," and is associated with the medical profession, specifically ethics. Although educators don't swear by an oath upon receiving licensure or accepting a childcare position, they do abide by a code of ethics that shares similar principles. The NAEYC *Code of ethical conduct and statement of commitment* (2005) states:

> Our paramount responsibility is to provide care and education in settings that are safe, healthy, nurturing, and responsive for each child. We are committed to supporting children's development and learning; respecting individual differences; and helping children learn to live, play, and work cooperatively. We are also committed to promoting children's self-awareness, competence, self-worth, resiliency, and physical well-being.
>
> (p. 2)

There is clearly a tension that exists for teachers of young children, who aspire to the NAEYC code of ethics in their daily work, but whose practices are being challenged by standards and legislation that feel contradictory in terms of being nurturing, respectful, and contributing to children's self-esteem. The legislators who drafted and approved the laws that contributed to the current high-stakes accountability climate believed that they were doing good, in efforts to close the achievement gap and strengthen teaching and schools. It is important to examine the politics of the No Child Left Behind Act as we continue to examine features of standardized testing.

No Child Left Behind Act

Almost immediately after his inauguration in January 2001, then President George W. Bush brought together a group of approximately 500 educators in the White House. There he unveiled his plan to improve American public education. Titled the No Child Left Behind Act, President Bush believed that this plan would usher in a "new era of high standards, testing, and accountability in which not a single child would be overlooked" (Ravitch, 2010, p. 93). In her book, *The death and life of the great American school system* (2010), Ravitch notes the irony in the choice of name for the legislation, borrowing the name from the slogan for the Children's Defense Fund. Marion Wright Edelman—president of CDF—created the slogan "Leave No Child Behind" in order to garner support for efforts targeted at reducing the number of children living in poverty in the United States. The NCLB legislation did not address poverty, nor consider it as a variable underlying children's school performance and later happiness and success.

Essentially a revised version of previous federal legislation, specifically the Elementary and Secondary Education Act of 1965, NCLB was approved, and subsequently signed into federal law on January 8, 2002. It's hard to succinctly capture political processes, but suffice it to say that both Democrats and Republicans supported the NCLB legislation. Democrats, such as Edward Kennedy (MA), praised NCLB because it provided for an expansion of the government's role in education. Public education deserves government support. Republicans, such as John Boehner (OH), approved of NCLB and its emphasis on accountability and freedom of choice of schools as warranted. Both government parties believed that the new focus on accountability would systematically coordinate education efforts and raise student achievement.

NCLB was not just an idea intended to spark enthusiasm and motivate educators and families. Table 4.2 presents several key features of the requirements attached to NCLB. The legislation was designed to systematically impact public education practices, and the way to ensure that the practices were indeed having the desired impact on students' learning was, and is, standardized assessment. However, individual states were given the flexibility to select their own tests to measure progress, and to define what progress meant in that state. The most pronounced pressure that came out of NCLB was its legislative mandate that all students in every public school must be "proficient" in mathematics and reading by the year 2014. This type of pressure is precisely what fuels the trickle-down reality of traditional assessment for children at younger ages, in earlier grades.

Table 4.2 Select Features of Accountability Under No Child Left Behind

All states are required to demonstrate annual student achievement through "Adequate Yearly Progress" (AYP), working toward a goal of 100 percent proficiency.

Children who attend public schools that have not made AYP for 2 or more consecutive years and have been designated schools in need of improvement (SINI) may transfer to a more successful school (increasingly punitive measures related to school choice include the school paying for transferring students' transportation out of federal funds; after 3 years the school must offer free tutoring to low-income students; after 4 years the school must take action to correct curriculum, staff, or elements of the school routine).

All states must develop and put into practice annual tests of reading and mathematics, determining proficiency on an individual state level.

All states are required to participate in the National Assessment of Educational Progress (NAEP) in reading and mathematics for grades 4 and 8, every other year. These scores provide a common measure against which to gauge states' progress.

Schools must separate students' scores by race, ethnicity, exceptionalities (e.g., disabilities, limited English language proficiency), and socioeconomic status.

Adapted from Ravitch (2010) & Essex (2006).

And so with the clock ticking, educators and school systems began administering exams in an effort to reach the goal of 100 percent proficiency. Needless to say, achieving 100 percent success in virtually any endeavor is impossible, and so the effort became rife with frustrated administrators, stifled teachers, and confused and deflated children and families. Very real, punitive consequences have resulted from the lack of success in achieving annual progress, let alone 100 percent proficiency. These include: the closing of neighborhood schools, the firing of teachers and principals (including many creative, collaborative educators), and the privatization of numerous public schools deemed beyond hope for improvement.

Research has more than suggested that NCLB is not the solution for underachieving schools. States are now being asked to adopt common-core curriculum standards that will be aligned with common tests, thus eliminating states' individual decisions around standards and proficiency. In a recent article, Ronald Wolk (2011, p. 24) raised some questions that appeal to our common sense:

- Why is it necessary to increase the use of testing when we know from years of previous testing what the results will be?
- Why make standards more rigorous when experience has consistently shown that student performance does not improve much?

Although the new common standards are indeed improvements for many states, Wolk cautions that "they will increase only standardization, not student learning" (p. 24).

A Letter From the President

Recently, President Barack Obama composed a letter to American citizens, explaining his plan for school improvement and reform, in which he states the "Blueprint for reauthorization of the Elementary and Secondary Education Act is not only a plan to renovate a flawed law, but also an outline for a reenvisioned federal role in education" (Obama, 2011). Included in the blueprint are plans to promote teacher collaboration and leadership, acknowledge the role of families and communities in children's education ("because a parent is a child's first teacher"), and support families, communities, and schools working in partnership in the interest of students' needs.

As altruistic as the letter may be, the tone fuels the public perception of public education as a failed system. Instead of promoting access and equal opportunities through funding for schools in high-poverty communities, it perpetuates the competitive race for funding as determined by and awarded to schools with evidence of children's progress—traditional test results.

Critics of the effort to improve the No Child Left Behind Act through implementation of the federal Race to the Top initiative warn against the over-reliance on test scores for monitoring accountability regarding children, teachers, and schools. "We need to make sure tests are valid, that is, they measure what they were designed to measure" (Kastner, 2011, p. 40). Understanding terms relating to standardized testing is fundamental to entering a dialogue about the use and benefits of traditional testing for young children. In the sections that follow, several terms are defined in order to provide a common understanding of the testing vernacular, and in the interest of recognizing what is, and is not, suitable for early childhood assessment.

Objectivity vs. Subjectivity

There is often a misunderstanding about standardized tests being objective measures, and therefore more desirable in gathering accurate information about young children. In fact, a false dichotomy exists between objectivity and subjectivity. Rather, it is helpful to consider them as opposite ends of a continuum, and to recognize that there is no purely objective test and no purely subjective measurement. Depending on the type of judgment that an educator is being asked to make, then the most appropriate method for making intelligent decisions is selected. For example, many standardized assessments include multiple-choice questions—items that have one correct answer—that are scored electronically. Other examples of objective test items include true/false and matching items. These types of questions limit the options for responses by providing a select number of choices for the correct answer.

One common criticism about such objective items is that there is often subjectivity on the part of the person who creates the test questions— choosing the range of possible responses, and determining which one is correct. Two different people could argue that two possible answers are correct, based on their own opinions and biases. In some cases, teachers are able to override a test answer key if they deem a different answer acceptable, but in the case of high-stakes standardized testing this is not possible, lending support to concerns about test biases. Subjectivity, on the other hand, allows for personal opinion to influence any judgments made. It is unlikely that someone could ever be exclusively subjective, as there are so many general facts about children's knowledge and abilities that many people would agree that a performance is above average or sub-par.

Because testing is present to such a strong degree in public education today, it is more critical that teachers understand the terms involved in interpreting, evaluating, and communicating test results. The terms below are incorporated into objective and subjective measures. Depending on the goals and methods of assessment, educators are more or less concerned with specific terms, but standardized testing typically infers greater reliance on the terms presented.

Reliability

Reliability refers to the consistency and stability involved in testing. Over time, a reliable test produces accurate, dependable scores. Educators are therefore able to generalize those scores to other test situations or other populations of children. The notion that individual evaluators would agree with each other is known as inter-rater reliability. Different teachers administering a test to their classes in two different states would score the children's performances within a desired rate of agreement, based on the type of questions asked and limited range of responses. Intra-rater reliability refers to one person administering and evaluating a test consistently, applying the same scoring criteria each time.

Validity

Validity refers to how well a standardized test measures what it is designed to measure. There are different considerations that determine validity, including:

- Face validity—a test appears to test what it claims to test (e.g. math tests should include math problems).
- Content validity—the test questions are appropriate (e.g. a first grade writing test includes an essay question about first grade content, not college-level astronomy).
- Predictive validity—the test scores can be used to predict a child's future performance (e.g. a kindergarten reading test in September predicts a child's reading level in May).

Population

A population is a group of individuals, in this case children, on which a test is administered in a systematic way, in order to reduce the larger population to a smaller sample of individuals whose scores are therefore representative of the larger population. Age, sex, socioeconomic status, and other demographic factors of a sample population are important to consider when selecting a test. The goal is that the scores from a sample can be used as a comparison for other groups that take the same test.

Norms

Norms is the term used to mean the scores that are gathered as a result of testing the sample group. A teacher can have confidence that norms are accurate if the population that was used to obtain the norms is similar to the population of students with whom she works. There is ongoing discussion about cultural sensitivity with respect to early childhood assessment, and this will be discussed in detail in Chapter 7.

Percentile Ranks

These scores are helpful in understanding how an individual child performed on a test, compared to a normative (sample) group. They are scores that result from the number of people in the sample group who answered correctly on the same number of questions. This is not the same as a percentage, meaning what percent of questions were answered correctly. Rather, a percentile ranking of 93 means that a child scored as well or better than 93 percent of the children in the sample group, not that she correctly answered 93 percent of the questions.

Rubrics

A rubric is a set of guidelines or scoring criteria for a test or piece of work. Rubrics are used to score from lowest to highest levels. Although rubrics are typically designed using a point scale, they can also contain descriptive language about what determines each level of quality.

Screening

Screening tests are short tests designed to provide educators with a relatively quick understanding of the developmental abilities of a particular group. Kindergarten screening is a routine part of most public schools, for example. Children are assessed for math and literacy knowledge and skills, as well as vision and hearing. Based on the results of the screening for an individual child, a teacher is able to make recommendations for classroom support or further assessment as deemed appropriate.

Diagnostic Testing

Diagnostic tests are specialized tests designed to gather information about a child's abilities. These are typically given in response to questions that have emerged from parents, teachers, or other specialists who notice that a child's abilities or behavior appear quite different from other children of the same age and grade. As a result of diagnostic assessment, a team meets to develop a plan to provide a child with optimal support for classroom success.

Classroom teachers often grapple with the pressures and requirements associated with traditional tests, and the tension between desired objectivity and their own "gut" instincts about children's abilities. The following case study illustrates a common scenario related to standardized testing and the uniqueness of individual children.

Case Study: A Level of Respect

Fresh out of her master's program in Early Childhood Education, Joanne is eager to apply the creative strategies she developed in many of her classes in her role as the new kindergarten teacher at the Mindess Elementary School. On the first day of orientation for new teachers, Joanne is introduced to the *Fountas & Pinnell Benchmark Assessment System* and the *Developmental Reading Assessment (DRA2)*, which are the school's measures for assessing children's reading abilities throughout the school year. Joanne understands the benchmarks that are suggested through the Fountas & Pinnell framework, and how the DRA2 is a standardized reading test used to gauge a child's "instructional" level in reading. The reading specialist, Mary Beth, explains that it's important from a teaching perspective that teachers understand how they can adjust their teaching to the needs of the children. They are not as concerned with the children's "independent" reading levels, because those are not considered in district assessments of student progress.

Since Mary Beth is the only reading specialist for four kindergarten classes, four first-grade classes, and three second-grade classes, she can't possibly administer the DRA2 to all of the children in those grades. Therefore, Joanne and her fellow kindergarten teammates are told that they will need to administer the DRA2 in September and May, and they are welcome to administer it to their students at other times during the year if they want to learn more about students' progress. Joanne feels fairly confident that she will be able to carve out the time needed to have each of her 22 students read one or two selected passages and then retell what they've read.

***

During her student teaching practicum, Joanne had most often used running records to evaluate children's progress, and she had limited experiences with two different teachers and their respective strategies to score children's reading using standardized measures. Joanne knows that teachers use DRA2 results and information from other assessments to tell if students are at, above, or below grade level. Based on the leveled texts in the Fountas and Pinnell system, she feels comfortable placing individual children into different letter categories associated with each level (see Table 4.3). After two weeks of screening and assessments, Joanne has a rough understanding of where each child stands in terms of reading levels. She feels as though all of their reading time has been focused on the assessment material, and can't wait to read entire books with and for the children, based on their interests.

Because she wants to be as accurate as possible, and because she doubts the accuracy of her first time assessing a class full of children, Joanne sets up a meeting with the reading specialist to discuss what a typical reading level is for kindergarten students at Mindess Elementary. Mary Beth tells her that children most often fall somewhere between an "A" and a "C." Then, glancing in the hallway before speaking, Mary Beth lowers her voice and leans closer to Joanne, saying, "I really think it's inappropriate to score kids at that age, because they're emerging readers. Just support them where they are and look for growth over the year." She told Joanne to pay attention to things like phonemic awareness, structures, concepts in print, and core skills.

***

When May flowers are in bloom, Joanne knows it is time to begin the end-of-year reading assessments of her students. She has documented the gains the children have made in all areas of the curriculum formally and informally, and many parents have shared their personal delight with her—thanking her for the attention she pays to their child as an individual. After two more weeks of reading tests, Joanne is full of pride about her class's growth in reading. She is proud that no one ranked below a level C, and goes into the Staff Lounge to share her happiness with another teacher. She skips over to Ilandia, a first-grade teacher, and blurts out, "They all scored C or better!" Ilandia's eyebrows and the corners of her mouth turn downward after Joanne's proclamation. She says to Joanne, "They should be C-independent and D-instructional. They need to be at an I in first grade." Joanne feels like she has been punched in the stomach. As she leaves the room, she fights back tears, second-guessing her teaching methods that have resulted in such meager gains for her students, but also feeling like she's received mixed messages. On the one hand, Mary Beth has encouraged her to take a developmental perspective on the children's reading, and now Ilandia is saying that if the students aren't as high as they can be, then the school won't make the required progress.

***

Joanne decides to retest a few children whose progress she had noted over the latter part of the school year. One child, Ava, is one of the last children she had tested with the DRA2 this second time around. Ava had failed much of the comprehension, but Joanne knows that her strategies and technical reading are stronger. Joanne checks her records, and sees that her accuracy score was high, while the comprehension score was low. For the retest, Joanne decides to go with the nonfiction version of the assessment, hoping that, if she can get Ava to perform better, she will have shown fellow teachers, such as Ilandia, evidence of progress. During the retesting, Joanne gives Ava a bit more prompting than in the previous testing session. On several occasions, Ava starts to answer a question and suddenly stops. On several occasions, Joanne asks her additional questions that help Ava respond differently and complete the sections.

***

On her summer vacation, Joanne thinks about Ava and the testing experience. She comes to the conclusion that the artificial scenario was resulting in lower scores. Joanne knew that she could elicit higher comprehension from Ava using strategies that worked, because she considers many of the questions to be "dead-end," artificial questions that lead to simple, pat answers. She starts to think about other ways she can work with students to develop test-taking strategies, deciding that she shouldn't have to justify children's reading levels just because of pressure from teachers at the next level who might look down on so-called "underperform-ing" children.

Table 4.3 Reading Level Comparison

Grade level	Fountas-Pinnell System	DRA2
		A
Kindergarten	A	1
	B	2
	C*	3
First Grade	C*	4
	D	6
	E	8
	F	10
	G	12
	H	14
	I	16
Second Grade	J, K	20
	L, M	28

*C is a level attributed to both kindergarten and first grade

Teacher-created Assessments

As a result of conflicting emotions that result from the use of standardized tests, many teachers develop their own assessment tools to gather information about children's learning. Some teachers use their own assessment strategies as a way to balance what sometimes feels like a restaurant server's tray, laden with dinner service for twelve. Teacher-created assessments can fill gaps that standardized tests overlook or ignore, and offer some flexibility in terms of what teachers consider important information to retain.

"To succeed, students can't simply amass information (as important as that is); they must also weigh its value and use it to resolve conflicting opinions, offer solutions, and propose reasonable recommendations" (Schmoker & Graff, 2011, pp. 31–33).

Teachers also recognize that creating their own assessments helps them to be better teachers. They can design tests or other measures that provide feedback during a specific learning period, such as a curriculum unit, or over the course of a semester or an entire school year. Testing done while teaching and learning is in progress is known as formative assessment, while testing done at the end of a designated period is called summative assessment. Formative assessment provides information about how a teacher can modify her teaching and classroom environment to provide children with greater opportunities to experience success and demonstrate their achievement. This requires clarity on the part of teachers in terms of goals, process, and assessment.

Hesitation about or caution concerning teacher-created assessment often centers on reliability and validity. Because teachers do not typically go through the rigorous processes required of standardized instruments, there is a greater risk of subjectivity and bias influencing the scores or outcomes of teacher-created tests. Two examples are provided in Figures 4.1 and 4.2, respectively, to illustrate how one first-grade teacher used her own tests to assess a student's (Claudia's) spelling and skills.

The first example, Figure 4.1, is an example of a spelling test given to children in order to assess their abilities spelling the designated words. Figure 4.2 extends this spelling experience a bit more, requiring the children to spell a different list of words correctly AND use the words in a sentence. Looking at the two spelling tests, what do you notice?

What are the implicit and explicit goals of the teacher? What are the implicit and explicit goals of first-grader Claudia? Are they the same? Did Claudia succeed, and how can you tell?

Another example from this same teacher is seen in Figure 4.3. In this case, the teacher did not create the specific test, but used a commercially

Figure 4.1
Spelling Test

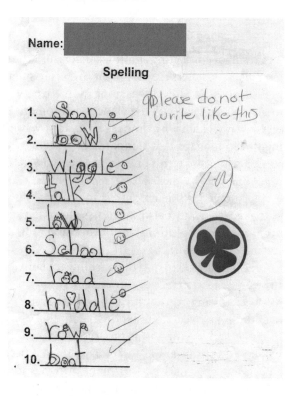

Name:

Spelling

please do not
write like this

1. Soap
2. bowl
3. Wiggle
4. talk
5. law
6. School
7. read
8. middle
9. raw
10. boot

produced math test to assess her students' math skills. In this case, the creative element is in how the teacher, Mrs. H, used the tool. She gave the first-graders one minute to answer the 36 math questions, and taught the students to keep track of how many problems they were able to complete at the end of the minute by writing the number at the top of the page. In this case, Claudia wrote "five" on the line above "Test Your Skills," but then erased it, and instead wrote "Don't show mom" underneath. She was given time during recess to complete the remaining 31 math problems, for which she received the red "C," indicating she had completed the test correctly. What are the implicit and explicit goals for the teacher? [Note: This is a math fluency test, according to the fine print at the bottom of the page.] What are the implicit and explicit goals for Claudia? How can you tell?

When teacher-created assessments are not bound to the scrutiny and rigor associated with standardized measures, there is room for wide variation in instructional practices, expectations for children's perform-ance, and the image of the child that is perpetuated in classroom practices and viewed through a narrow lens.

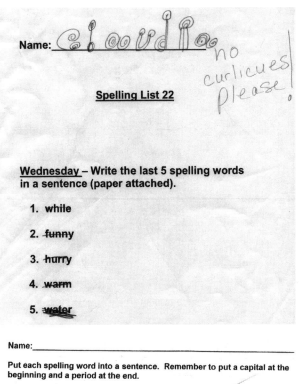

Figure 4.2
Spelling Test
with Sentences

Name: *Cloudia*

no curlicues please!

Spelling List 22

Wednesday – Write the last 5 spelling words
in a sentence (paper attached).

1. while

2. funny

3. hurry

4. warm

5. water

Name:_____

Put each spelling word into a sentence. Remember to put a capital at the
beginning and a period at the end.

① Can we go to the park for a while.

② You are not funny.

③ Please harry or you will be late.

④ I will be warm.

⑤ I like the water.

Figure 4.3
Math Test

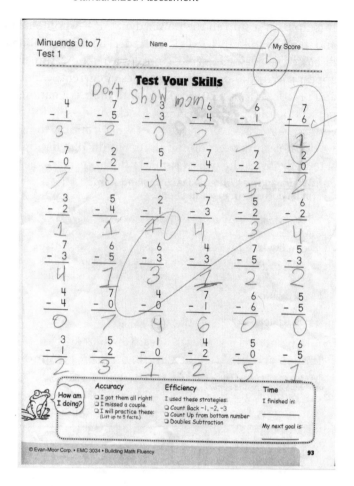

Paradigm Shifts and Cultural Shifts

A quote from educator Sir Ken Robinson sums up the negative sentiments associated with standardized testing, while expressing a desire to refocus the assessment lens:

> It's not that I am against standardized testing. What I've personally got a rant about is the extent to which standardized testing, firstly, has become a massive commercial industry which is detached, in most cases, from the real purpose of education. And secondly, the extent to which we've come to associate standardizing with raising standards. Now, everybody agrees we should raise standards in schools. Of course you should. But, the primary instrument that's being used is standardized testing. And the problem with it is that it fails to do the one thing we know works if we want to improve standards in schools, which is to address personal development.

(Robinson, 2009)

It is time for a shift in the power dynamic—who holds the knowledge and how that knowledge is shared. The accountability movement, discussed in Chapter 1, serves "mostly to make dreadful forms of teaching appear successful" according to critics of current school reform policies and practices (Kohn, 2011, p. 34). Until there is a nationwide shift in the perception of what matters most for children—the future leaders of our country—and a reconsideration of what it means to be a citizen of the world, not simply economic units within our nation's borders, then standardized testing will continue to be the primary means under which children are assessed.

In President Obama's letter, cited earlier, he states:

> A generation ago, we led all nations in college completion, but today, ten countries have passed us. It is not that their students are smarter than ours. It is that these countries are being smarter about how to educate their students. And the countries that out-educate us today will out-compete us tomorrow.
>
> (Obama, 2011)

If the implications for the President's words weren't so serious, then they would be perfect for a Shakespearean comedy. One Merriam-Webster definition of comedy is "the genre of dramatic literature dealing with the comic or serious in a light or satirical manner." The comedy, or perhaps irony, is that amidst the fear about other nations out-educating and out-competing us, two of the nations who out-scored the United States with international standardized test results believe that structuring schools around testing is not such a good thing!

Global Response

South Korea's former minister of education, science, and technology, Byong Man Ahn, has warned the United States about imitating his country's approach to educating young students. From his vantage point, he argues that the South Korean approach has grown overly focused on tests, thereby taking away from students' love of learning. Forcing students to memorize factual information has resulted in students experiencing learning as an unpleasant, pressured regimen instead of one that results in joy as a natural extension of participating in and constructing learning experiences (Cavanagh, 2011).

Similarly, citizens in another Asian nation that outperformed the United States on global achievement tests has begun to recognize the deficits that result from an emphasis on testing in children's education. In the wake of math scores that topped the charts on the Program for

International Student Assessment (PISA) test, educators in China have acknowledged that their society is successful at generating "mid-level accountants, computer programmers and technocrats" but that they subsequently struggle to produce the innovative thinkers and entrepreneurs needed to sustain the current global economy. The most promising students in China still travel abroad to other countries "to develop their managerial drive and creativity, and there they have to unlearn the test-centric approach to knowledge that was drilled into them" (Xueqin, 2011).

Achievement 101

As politicians engage in discussions about how to build the best federal plans for accountability, researchers, educators, and child advocates continue to voice concerns about the use of standardized tests to raise achievement. A study conducted by a committee of the National Academies' National Research Council examined various incentives such as NCLB requirements, high school exit exams, and teacher merit-pay programs. The committee's findings support evaluation and accountability, but determined that "the approaches implemented so far have had little or no effect on actual student learning, and in some cases have run counter to their intended purposes" (Sparks, 2011, p. 1). Other investigations have revealed reporting practices that are misleading, prompting a need for closer attention paid to "who is tested and who is not" when making assumptions about progress as a result of increased testing (Haney, 2006, p. 7). Perhaps a return to basics is needed.

There is a growing body of research that supports a systematic approach to recognizing the ways standard practices include material that is not common in the majority of American classrooms. For example, one recent study provides scientific evidence that The 4Rs (reading, writing, respect, and resolution) have a powerful effect on children academically, but also emotionally (Jones, Brown, & Aber, 2011). Students in this study made significant academic gains as a result of school-wide participation in one class every week, in which students engaged in reading, writing, discussion, and skills practice aimed at fostering caring, responsible, behavior.

In a self-study of her own school environment, Linda Nathan (2009) describes how the Boston Arts Academy (a public high school with an arts focus) has increased students' overall achievement and college acceptance rate. This is remarkable in a school with demographics that include an almost 80 percent minority student body, and 60 percent who meet the criteria for free or reduced lunch. The school community has created specific frameworks for intellectual and social goals, based on information Nathan and staff gain after in-depth, detailed questioning of students. The staff learn about the needs and aspirations of the broader school community, and can create and modify curricula accordingly. The result is that students become more invested in the school's mission. The power of relationships that has been stressed throughout this book has the potential to impact children's school success and the racial achievement gap that is the focus of education policies.

Other studies echo the success of programs that address the achievement gap as an opportunity to engage students in learning experiences, rather than merely accepting discrepancies in knowledge and skills among social groups as unwavering fact. Researchers have found that reframing the achievement gap as an empowerment gap gives students "a sense of their own power and ability to affect change for themselves and others around them" (Berman, 2010, p. 1). When students' access to curricula is broadened rather than narrowed, students' motivation increases. If such motivation is nurtured in children in early childhood classrooms and throughout the education spectrum, there is strong evidence that the culture currently focused on standardized tests as the answer would change dramatically. The focus on personalized rather than standardized assessment and curriculum is one of the driving forces behind authentic assessments, to be discussed in the next chapter.

Summary

This chapter provides information about the complex practice of using standardized tests to assess young children's learning. There are many challenges that impact the daily classroom lives of children, teachers, and families. As the federal government responds to decades of school reform efforts and revised legislation, traditional assessments provide a relatively quick, objective way to gain information about children's academic progress. Depending on the goals of standardized assessment, specific elements are important to consider, and therefore familiarity with testing language is fundamental to accurate measurement. Teachers frequently experience a tension between following standardized procedures and following their gut instincts where individual children are concerned. This prompts some practitioners to develop their own testing tools, and there is a risk that subjectivity and bias may impact the assessment system in an unbalanced way. In order to minimize potential damage to a child's self-esteem and self-image as a competent learner, many educators support the use of alternative assessment measures that are more authentic.

Now What?

1. What is most important for a teacher to know about a child's abilities in the classroom? Which physical, cognitive, and social skills are most critical to classroom success?
2. Various forms of standardized assessment exist to provide information to teachers and families. What role should the government play in determining how many assessments are necessary to gain a clear picture of a child's abilities?
3. Despite the negative attention resulting from the intense pressures associated with standardized testing, educators do agree that evaluation and accountability are important. How is our level of comfort with assessment influenced by perceptions of our standing compared to other countries?

Avenues for Inquiry

Sir Ken Robinson

The link below brings you to a video of a talk given by education advocate and author, Sir Ken Robinson. In this talk, he proposes a radical shift in educational practice, moving away from standardized practices to more personalized educational experiences.

　　http://www.ted.com/talks/sir_ken_robinson_bring_on_the_revolution. html

alfiekohn.org

This website features links to articles about standardized testing and strategies to help American schools. There is a link to the homepage where visitors can find scores of articles and other materials written by Alfie Kohn in the areas of education, parenting, and human development in general.

　　www.alfiekohn.org/stdtest.htm

Linda Darling-Hammond

This link brings you to a video clip in which Linda Darling-Hammond discusses international assessments and standards from a global perspective. She discusses educational practices in other countries, and offers examples that educators and policymakers in the United States should consider in terms of what is truly important to be competitive on an international level.

http://www.edutopia.org/international-teaching-learning-assessment-video

5

Authentic Assessment

Advocates for authentic, contextualized data should persuade policy makers (or their delegates) to take the necessary viewing time, to set policy by viewing live action instead of reading static numbers. Although numbers can help in other areas, such as teacher-child ratios, average income, ethnic mix, absenteeism, body weight, and so forth, these are rather distal indicators of quality.
(Forman, 2010, p. 31)

Authentic assessment can be defined in numerous ways, for a variety of purposes, and communicate a range of meanings. A quick investigation using the Microsoft Word dictionary feature generates the following definition for "authentic": 1) not false or copied, 2) trustworthy, and 3) valid, with synonyms "genuine" and "real." Several of these words are commonly used in defense of standardized assessments, which lends support to the argument that authentic assessments and standardized assessments are complementary practices, working in the shared interest of identifying what young children know and can do.

Many educators, particularly those who work in early childhood education, view alternative assessment as a "developmentally appropriate alternative to conventional tests and testing practices" (Bagnato, 2009, p. vii). This opinion is especially strong among educators—novices and veterans—who strongly believe (based on personal experience or empathy) that traditional tests too often result in misperceptions about children's abilities and competence. Authentic assessments actualize the significance of assessing each unique child's knowledge and behavior, as well as learning style, over time. Compared to a standardized test that captures a child's performance on a specific day, authentic assessment provides more than a snapshot of children's understanding and capabilities. This means that knowledge of child development and the effects of many environmental factors are central considerations when defining a child's performance using authentic assessment.

The challenge that often feels overwhelming to early childhood educators is the necessary effort required to balance what they know about children's individual differences (e.g. temperament, learning styles, culture, primary spoken language), uphold designated standards, and maximize opportunities for all children to succeed. Fortunately, authentic assessment is more flexible than standardized assessment, because authentic assessment practices incorporate various assessment strategies and goals within the assessment process. This leaves room for adjustments that provide greater opportunities for children's abilities to be made visible. For example, authentic assessment welcomes multiple perspectives and collaboration, which makes it possible for a multi-dimensional image of a child to emerge, considering input from children, families, teachers, and other experts. This is quite different from a flat, two-dimensional account based on one single moment in time. For a better understanding of what this actually looks like in practice, the second website link in the "Avenues for Inquiry" section of this chapter provides an excellent example of what authentic assessment looks like in one particular classroom context.

On a Personal Level

Because individual talents and abilities are made visible through authentic assessments, people often refer to such tools under the category "personalized education." Some experts argue that if the citizens of our country are truly committed to leaving no child behind, then personalized education, not standardized experiences, is a more promising, energizing force behind that effort. Schools should be measured on a human scale (Wolk, 2011), not simply with numerical data. This is relevant to early childhood education, as well as education at all levels, for many reasons.

In terms of relationships, which have been shown time and again to be the most significant factor in children's successful, healthy development, personalized education would foster school environments in which children and teachers get to know each other very well. Such "growth-promoting" relationships provide children "what nothing else in the world can offer—experiences that are individualized to the child's unique personality style; that build on his or her own interests, capabilities, and initiative; that shape the child's self-awareness; and that stimulate the growth of his or her heart and mind" (NSCDC, 2004, p. 1). Table 5.1 compares some advantages and disadvantages of using authentic assessment in the classroom.

Table 5.1 Advantages and Disadvantages of Authentic Assessment

Advantages	Disadvantages
Emphasis on critical thinking and application of knowledge	Greater chance for bias, subjectivity
Fosters creativity and individuality	Takes greater amount of time to organize and manage
Appropriate for individuals and collaborative groups	Challenging to map onto required state and federal standards
Assessment, instruction, and learning objectives are aligned	Grading processes may be inconsistent
Encourages multiple skill sets from a variety of domains	Non-traditional format may be challenging for children who prefer more structure

Understanding the benefits of authentic assessment does not mean condemning other forms of assessment. In an interview, assessment expert Grant Wiggins attempted to clear up any misunderstanding about the value of authentic assessment, and placing all hopes for student achievement in authentic evaluations alone:

> There's a lot of authentic work that doesn't make for good assessment because it's so messy and squishy and it involves so many different people and so many variables that you can't say with any certainty, "Well what did that individual know about those particular objectives in this complex project that occurred over a month?" So there's a place for unauthentic, non-real-world assessments. We're just making the distinction that you shouldn't leave school not knowing what big people actually do.
>
> (Wiggins, 2011)

The desire to be certain that children leave school knowing certain things is slightly more complicated in early childhood assessment, because "big people" (parents, teachers, administrators, legislators) want to be sure children are "ready to learn" before they enter formal schooling. Measures are incorporated into daily routines in preschool classrooms so that teachers gain a sense of school readiness by the time kindergarten beckons. Teachers of young children know from their child development classes, if not instinct, that children are *born* ready to learn. They understand that the real "task is not to make children ready for schools, but to make schools ready for children" (Mardell et al., 2010, p. 45).

On a Professional Level

This hasn't softened the impact of assessments or classroom require-ments. It is therefore vital that authentic assessments be conducted with thoughtful planning, clear goals and expectations, and instructional activities that guide children's performance and provide opportunities for improvement. Knowing about some of the different options allows teachers to match the best authentic assessment experiences with goals for children's understanding, and to collaborate with colleagues, children, and families to gather information. The examples below provide a sam-pling of assessments that fall under the authentic assessment umbrella.

Portfolio Assessment

A portfolio is a compilation of student work gathered over time, docu-menting growth in particular curriculum areas. Portfolios are often publicly shared, among children and with families and the school com-munity, to showcase students' improvement and work the teacher and/or child are proud to share. Portfolios are also used to illustrate how a child's work meets specific educational standards. Throughout the process of gathering, considering, and selecting pieces of representative work, the child develops skills in self-regulation and delay of gratification. Portfolios also provide insight into students' intrinsic motivation, per-severance, and effort. Portfolios are sometimes included in standardized assessments, such as the *Work Sampling System* (Meisels et al., 2001), which many teachers find appealing because of the elements of authentic assessment that contribute to a more well-rounded understanding of a child's development.

Performance Assessment

"Performance assessment" is a broad term used often because of the mandates that require evidence of children's annual academic progress. In the context of authentic assessment, performance assessments measure children's abilities to demonstrate knowledge skills in an organic, relevant way. Performance assessments are particularly helpful when academic goals include a specific behavioral component or the acquisition of acade-mic and social skills that are best judged under specific circumstances.

Group Assessment and Exploration

In the everyday world that exists outside of classroom settings, people tend to realize that many heads are better than one when trying to solve a problem or reach a desired goal. When children are grouped into small groups of between three and six children, they are able to explore ideas and concepts while simultaneously developing social skills and strengthening relationships. Children are able to utilize skills that help them identify questions or hypotheses, describe what they see and do, document their experiences, and make predictions about future investigations. Authentic group activities therefore provide opportunities for assessment of social and academic skills, which require the application of prior knowledge to solve problems and learn new information.

Self-Assessment

Self-assessments provide opportunities for children to develop reflective, mindful practices. They take a closer look at their own thinking and learning, areas of strength, and identify areas for growth. The goals of self-assessments include the development of skills for reflection, self-monitoring and correction of errors, evaluation, and revising work in progress. Examples of self-assessments include journals, photographs, video clips, audio recordings, and drawings. The ability to reflect on their progress and products empowers children to understand and control the outcomes of their work, measured against a clear, structured rubric or set of guidelines.

Authentic assessments open lines of communication between teachers and children, and with families, and make specific learning goals transparent. Key to the use of authentic assessment is a teacher's clarity around the underlying values being transmitted throughout the assessment process.

Balancing Idealism and Reality

Teachers of young children understand that children's development may make it difficult for individual children to succeed at a desired task. Depending on a child's needs or repertoire of skills, a teacher may need to adjust materials, classroom layout, or the manner in which information is presented. In the context of increasing demands on children and teachers, "[e]ducators need to figure out what values are being rewarded in the classroom, articulate those values, and reinforce them without embarrassment or apology" (Boris-Schacter, 2001, p. 43). Teachers need to establish their own sense of equilibrium between accountability and the reality of what the children in their classroom are capable of producing. In the example that follows, consider the following questions as you read artifacts from one teacher's attempt at authentic assessment: What explicit goals are apparent from the teacher's instructions and scoring rubric? What questions might a caregiver have after reading the instructions, rubric, and list of ideas? Are the teacher's expectations realistic for six- and seven-year-olds?

First Grade Book Report

A first grade teacher, Ms. S, sent home a packet of materials for parents to read about an assigned book report, which contained the following pages:

- The cover sheet (note—the words below are printed precisely as they were presented on the assignment sheet):

  I am assigning a book report this quarter. Your child is to pick a book to do their project on. It can be a pick from home, a library book or even one of the free books the children have been given here at school. The child must read the book or you read the book to them.

  Next, they MUST fill out the book report form NEATLY (see attached).

  Finally, they must do an art project to go along with the book. They can do a diorama (a shoebox with a scene from the story), make a puppet or create a poster. (See the list of ideas from the attached list).

  No late projects will be accepted!

- The Book Report Response Sheet, reproduced from a commercial product similar to Figure 5.1.
- The Book Report Grading Sheet (Figure 5.2).
- The 35-item *List of Ideas* that M referred to in the assignment description (Figure 5.3).

The example described above is not uncommon, as teachers attempt to stretch children's capabilities to meet higher demands or expectations. On one hand, the list of suggested ideas in Figure 5.3 contains activities that, considered alone, are indeed authentic experiences in that they ask students to undertake real tasks that will provide solid, life-long skills. On the other hand, they are much better suited for older children and

I like
ice
cream!

Name
_____
– – – – – – – – – – – – – – – – – –
_____

Date
_____
– – – – – – – – – – –
_____

Title
_____
– – – – – – – – – – – – – – – – – –
_____

Author
_____
– – – – – – – – – – – – – – – – – –
_____

Write two sentences about the book.

_____
– – – – – – – – – – – – – – – – – –
_____

_____
– – – – – – – – – – – – – – – – – –
_____

_____
– – – – – – – – – – – – – – – – – –
_____

Where does the story happen?
_____
– – – – – – – – – – – – – – –
_____

_____
– – – – – – – – – – – – – – –
_____

This story
takes
place on a
farm!

Figure 5.1 Book Report Sheet

Name:_____

Book Report Grading Sheet

Figure 5.2
Book Report
Grading Sheet

A – the project came in on time. The coloring was done neatly. The report was filled out.

B – the project came in on time. The coloring was OK, but could have been better. The report was filled out.

C – the project did not come in at all or only one piece came in.

Grade:_____
Comments:_____
_____
_____

contain references to many unfamiliar and inappropriate concepts for first graders. For example, suggestion number seven mentions "Dear Abby," number thirteen suggests a persuasive essay, number fifteen uses the term "card catalogue," and number eighteen mentions abstract writing terms that children are supposed to create by extracting suitable words from the book. It is confusing to identify learning goals from these materials, although neatness is clearly important in both writing and coloring. While the book report assignment has the potential for real learning, the framing of the assignment (directed to parents) and the juxtaposition of child-friendly worksheet and developmentally inappropriate activities make the process and evaluation rather muddled and ineffective.

BOOK REPORT IDEAS

1. Make a diorama depicting a scene from the book.   Write a sentence(s) /paragraph(s) to describe your scene.
2. Make a bookmark with title and author on the front. On the back, write a sentence telling about the book.
3. Pretend you are a reporter for a newspaper. Write a news story about something which happened in the book.
4. Write an outline for your book.
5. Make a papier-mache' or clay figure of your favorite character. Write a descriptive paragraph.
6. Devise a plan for rating books.,i.e. numbers, color codes, etc.
7. Write a "Dear Abby" letter from the point of view of the main character. The class answers the letter.
8. Write a letter of advice to one of the story characters.
9. Compose a telegram, giving the main idea of the story, in fifteen words or less.
10. Write a letter to a friend recommending the book.
11. Write a letter to the author telling how much you enjoyed the book.
12. Write an interview with the main character.
13. Write a speech to persuade others to read the book.
14. Write a biography for one of the characters.
15. Write a "card catalogue" entry card for the book.
16. Create riddles from new vocabulary words in the book.
17. Write a character sketch of one person in the book.
18. Create metaphors, similes, personifications, alliteration, hyperbole, or idioms, using words from the book.
19. Write statements of facts and opinions from the book. Use as an oral or written exercise.
20. Write a framed paragraph about the book.
21. Write a poem or song to describe the book.
22. Write a paragraph that describes the setting of the story.
23. Write a short play, using characters in the book.
24. Compare and contrast two story characters from the same author.
25. Create a rebus for the book.
26. Write headlines summarizing events in the book.
27. Rewrite the ending of the book.
28. Make a word search or crossword puzzle, using vocabulary words from the book.
29. Write a dialogue between two characters.
30. Write directions to a new game, using the characters and events in the book.
31. Make a mobile which includes main character, setting, and main events of the book.
32. Make a time line depicting the sequence of events in the story.
33. Write a book review for the class newspaper.
34. Make a cartoon depicting an event in the book.
35. Design and write a postcard home telling about an adventure in the book.

Figure 5.3 List of Ideas

Project Spectrum

In contrast to the long-prevailing view of intelligence as a singular, you've-either-got-it- or-you-don't ability focused on math and language skills, the Project Spectrum approach to assessment of young children recognizes the theory of multiple intelligences proposed by Howard Gardner (1983). The theory of multiple intelligences recognizes children's competence in many areas, such as music, movement, and interpersonal domains. As a result of a collaboration between educators at Harvard and Tufts Universities, the Project Spectrum approach is an attempt to reconceptualize traditional assessment and the narrow views of intelligence that serve as the foundation for most traditional assessment tools. Although many assessment instruments are designed on the assumption that children progress in a uniform, predictable way through general stages of development, the Project Spectrum approach was designed to recognize variation among individuals and classroom activities (Krechevsky, 1991).

Notable features of the Project Spectrum assessment approach include:

- blurring the line between curriculum and assessment by gathering information over time in the child's own environment;
- embedding assessment in meaningful, real-world activities;
- using measures that are "intelligence-fair";
- emphasizing children's strengths;
- attending to the stylistic dimensions of performance.

(p. 44)

Table 5.2 describes specific activities that fall under categories inspired by the theory of multiple intelligences. It is apparent that the experiences described represent a thoughtful array of typical, developmentally appropriate classroom activities, but here viewed through an assessment lens that the teacher can focus on individuals and groups of children.

A common criticism often associated with authentic forms of assessment—portfolio, performance, group/exploration, and self-assessment—is that such assessments are too time intensive, too costly, and too difficult for one teacher to handle. For teachers who are striving for personal and professional equilibrium, it is sometimes difficult to imagine the return on investments structuring and assessing classroom activities and experiences that build life-long skills that will transfer to adult situations and behavior.

Upon close inspection, many of the arguments voiced by hesitant teachers are not accurate. On the contrary, authentic assessment is not necessarily expensive, and is typically less costly than the purchase price

Table 5.2 Areas of Cognitive Ability Examined in Project Spectrum

Numbers

Dinosaur Game: Measures a child's understanding of number concepts, counting skills, ability to adhere to rules, and use of strategy.

Bus Game: Assesses a child's ability to create a useful notation system, perform mental calculations, and organize number information for one or more variables.

Science

Assembly Activity: Measures a child's mechanical ability. Successful completion of the activity depends on fine motor skills and visual-spatial, observational, and problem-solving abilities.

Treasure Hunt Game: Assesses a child's ability to make logical inferences. The child is asked to organize information to discover the rule governing the placement of various treasures.

Water Activity: Assesses a child's ability to generate hypotheses based on his or her observations and to conduct simple experiments.

Discovery Area: Includes year-round activities that elicit a child's observations, appreciation, and understanding of natural phenomena.

Music

Music Production Activity: Measures a child's ability to maintain accurate pitch and rhythm while singing and his or her ability to recall a song's musical properties.

Music Perception Activity: Assesses a child's ability to discriminate pitch. The activity consists of song recognition, error recognition, and pitch discrimination.

Language

Storyboard Activity: Measures a range of language skills including complexity of vocabulary and sentence structure, use of connections, use of descriptive language and dialogue, and ability to pursue a storyline.

Reporting Activity: Assesses a child's ability to describe an event he or she has experienced with regard to the following criteria: ability to report content accurately, level of detail, sentence structure, and vocabulary.

Visual Arts

Art Portfolios: The contents of a child's art portfolio are reviewed twice a year and assessed on criteria that include use of lines and shapes, color, space, detail, and representation and design. Children also participate in three structured drawing activities. The drawings are assessed on criteria similar to those used in the portfolio assessment.

Movement

Creative Movement: The ongoing movement curriculum focuses on children's abilities in five areas of dance and creative movement: sensitivity to rhythm, expressiveness, body control, generation of movement ideas, and responsiveness to music.

Table 5.2 Continued

Athletic Movement: An obstacle course focuses on the types of skills found in many different sports such as coordination, timing, balance, and power.

Social

Classroom Model Activity: Assesses a child's ability to observe and analyze social events and experiences in his or her classroom.

Peer Interaction Checklist: A behavioral checklist is used to assess the behaviors in which children engage when interacting with peers. Different patterns of behavior yield distinctive social roles such as facilitator and leader.

Source: Krechevsky (1991:45–46).

of a standardized assessment kit, requisite training, and analysis. Furthermore, in order to meet the standards set forth by NCLB and other legislation, there must be evidence of student progress. Assessments that include opportunities for performance-based data collection meet the requirement for obtaining children's progress, and can have an immediate connection to classroom instruction. Rather than detract from quality instruction or feel like multi-tasking, authentic assessment and collaboration serve to improve teachers' daily practices with children.

Collaboration

Recently, Chen and McNamee (2007) developed an authentic assessment approach similar, in some ways, to the Project Spectrum approach. Titled *Bridging* because of the explicit connections between authentic assessment and classroom instruction, *Bridging* acknowledges and values the variety of ways in which children demonstrate mastery and intelligence across the early childhood (ages 3–8) curriculum. The authors state that, "[t]eachers can use *Bridging* on their own, but it also holds great potential when used by teachers working together on an ongoing basis" (p. xiii).

The authors further note, "the insights gathered through the *Bridging* assessment process provide teachers with a language for articulating to professionals, colleagues, and parents what is happening in classrooms where there is joy, passion, commitment to learning, and intellectual challenge" (p. xiii). Many early childhood advocates cite an inability to communicate with policymakers as one of the greatest obstacles to affecting change in policy. The word "code-switching" is often used to describe the mindset that teachers in classrooms and legislators in government offices are speaking different languages. *Bridging* is therefore a bridge between early childhood classrooms and legislation, in addition to the bridges that are created between assessment and instruction.

The following two figures are examples of drawings children created in a *Bridging* activity entitled "Drawing a Self-Portrait". Six-year-old Talia drew Figure 5.4, and eight-year-old Matthew drew Figure 5.5. The instructions given to each child were the same, "Draw a picture of yourself at home," and embedded in casual conversation about drawing self-portraits. The directions also encouraged the children to include details in the picture that show the viewer where they are in their home and what that room looks like. Each child chose to draw her- and himself in their respective bedrooms. There was no time limit for this task, and, when the children indicated they were finished, they were each given the chance to change or add details and to describe their drawings.

The evaluation process is guided by several *Bridging* rubrics, which focus on evaluative working approach, descriptive working approach, and performance. As raters look at examples such as Figures 5.4 and 5.5 they score the children and then consider how the knowledge gained can inform classroom planning and instruction. Using this approach, the image of the child is one of an active participant in their own learning. The teacher learns about content and process—in other words, the

Figure 5.4 Talia's *Bridging* Drawing

Figure 5.5 Matthew's *Bridging* Drawing

"what" and "how" involved in learning on an individual basis. The goal for teachers is not to demonstrate scores in a specific range, but rather to enter into dialogue about children's learning, with the children, and with colleagues and families.

Bridging expands upon other authentic assessment practices by integrating assessment with teaching and learning. Documentation of children's performances on tasks that teachers select, aligned with performance standards teachers select, provides information about the progress of individual students and the group as a whole. Teachers use this information to plan lessons and experiences to extend learning for all students. Many aspects of the *Bridging* approach are similar to an approach that is being widely adopted in schools across the country, in response to a combination of desires—to identify early children who may need services and interventions; to reduce costs associated with providing those necessary supports; and to collaborate in the interest of best practices and student achievement.

Response to Intervention

Response to Intervention (RTI) is an approach that integrates assessment and intervention within a tiered or multi-level prevention system. The overarching goals are to increase student achievement and to lower the incidence of behavioral problems that hinder a child's learning in the classroom. The RTI approach feels more comfortable for many educators and administrators, because prior to RTI, schools and teachers wouldn't learn about challenges for some students until well into the school year, which meant that teachers' hands were sometimes tied in terms of advocating for special services or supports, and administrators were often pressured to keep the number of requests to a minimum in order to maintain a desired budget. The process is straightforward in theory, but more challenging in practice. Schools use screening data to identify students at risk for poor learning outcomes, monitor student progress, provide interventions and gather evidence that suggests an adjustment to the intensity and nature of those interventions or the cessation of the intervention. Depending on a student's responsiveness, further assessment may be warranted, and students may be identified with learning disabilities or other disabilities as a result of the process (NCRTI, 2010).

The driving force behind RTI is prevention. The approach makes direct links between assessment and instruction, which are intended to inform teachers' decisions about how best to teach their students. "A goal is to minimize the risk for long-term negative learning outcomes by responding quickly and efficiently to documented learning or behavioral problems and ensuring appropriate identification of students with disabilities" (p. 4).

While RTI was initially associated with special education and a method to increase proficiency for early readers, it is now incorporated into a variety of content areas and developmental considerations. Fans of the RTI approach have credited the process as making a significant difference in efforts to reduce the overall population of students diagnosed with specific learning disabilities. In the current economic climate, amidst consistent budget cuts, it is interesting to consider the fact that RTI materials are one expense for which more and more school districts advocate for increased spending (Samuels, 2011).

Figure 5.6 shows the relationship among essential components of RTI. Note the emphasis on data-based decision making represented in the center circle. The gathering of data (a.k.a., evidence) is essential for the other three components to function in an optimal way. All components must be implemented using culturally responsive and evidence-based practices. The basic RTI framework contains: 1) a school-wide, multi-level instructional and behavioral system for preventing school failure, 2) screening, 3) progress monitoring, 4) data-based decision making for instruction, movement within the multi-level system, and disability identification (in accordance with state law). This is vastly different than

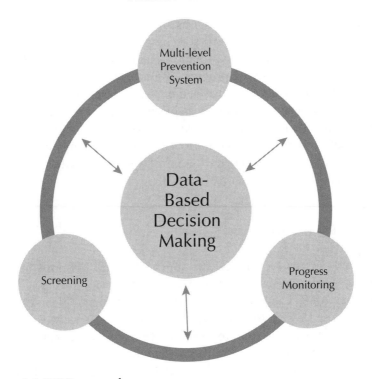

Figure 5.6 RTI Framework

giving students a standardized test and trying to identify any inconsistencies between a child's cognitive abilities and academic outputs (NCRTI, 2011).

Administrators' Perspective

Administrators recognize the benefits of RTI for children, but also acknowledge the support that RTI provides to teachers. First, RTI has potential for helping teachers and schools reach the federal NCLB goal of 100 percent student proficiency in reading and math by 2014. Also, when districts and schools use the RTI model they are addressing guidelines in the Individuals with Disabilities Education Act (IDEA) 2004, legislation that will be discussed in Chapter 7 (Galvin, 2007). The federal Education Department enforces individuals' rights, such as the idea that RTI can't be used to delay or deny a child's evaluation, and similarly that established processes and resources must continue to be discussed.

No time limit has been suggested by the federal Education Department in terms of how long individual states and districts can use RTI with students. Since the RTI approach was not designed to go on indefinitely, "cut points"—scores/results of a screening tool or progress monitoring tool—determine whether to provide a child with additional supports. For example, in terms of progress monitoring, the cut point helps educators decide if a student has demonstrated responsiveness, whether or not to make changes in classroom instruction, and whether to reduce the intensity of services and supports. A concern shared by some parents and teachers is that the RTI approach may keep some children at a relatively low level of support, without the appropriate education needs being accurately identified or addressed.

Parents' Perspective

Yet many parents are enthusiastic about what RTI has done for their children's educational experience and confidence (Kelleher, 2011). Supporters of RTI appreciate the focus on identifying problems early, the use of focused lessons to address students' challenges before they become deep-rooted patterns, and on the goal of improving education for all students (Samuels, 2011). Parents also like the way that RTI is available for all students, even students who aren't struggling with academics or behavior. The RTI framework provides high quality instruction that is culturally and linguistically responsive and aligned with state standards. "The high quality primary prevention should be effective and sufficient for about 80% of the student population" (NCRTI, 2010, p. 8).

As much as educational supporters and policymakers celebrate the benefits of RTI, it remains difficult to convince some parents. There is a contention among some parents that schools which use the RTI approach for identifying and serving students with learning deficits don't always provide interventions that work or do an adequate job explaining next steps if a suggested intervention doesn't work. Other parents claim that the RTI approach is implemented inconsistently across school districts. While inconsistent implementation is the most frequently reported concern about RTI, the other most consistent concern is that some parents feel RTI may hinder or prevent the process of identifying their children for services and supports.

The main element embedded in the RTI approach that appeals to both parents and teachers is the fact that the approach places such a strong focus on instruction. RTI looks directly at student achievement in a most fundamental way, prompting consideration and communication on behalf of children's learning.

Looking at Students' Work

In the second edition of their book, *Looking together at student work*, authors Blythe, Allen, & Powell (2007) provide examples and inspiration for teachers who wish to advocate for keeping students at the core of a meaningful evaluation process. They describe an assessment protocol in which a group of teachers come together and engage in a systematic approach to looking at students' work, while strengthening their skills in professional collaboration. Through this process teachers discover what students' work conveys about individual students, and relevant issues that pertain to the students' interests and strategies. Through close analysis and discussion, teachers learn together how the qualities that contribute to students' work align with the goals that the students' teachers have for their progress. The Collaborative Assessment Conference described in Table 5.3 provides a helpful structure for groups of teachers to focus on classroom instruction, anchored in students' work.

Table 5.3 The Collaborative Assessment Conference

I. Getting started
- The group chooses a facilitator who will make sure the group stays focused on the particular issue addressed in each step.
- The presenting teacher puts the selected work in a place where everyone can see it or provides copies for the other participants. S/he says nothing about the work, the context in which it was created, or the student until Step V.
- The participants observe or read the work in silence, perhaps making brief notes about aspects of it that they particularly notice.

II. Describing the work
- The facilitator asks the group, "What do you see?"
- Group members provide answers without making judgments about the quality of the work or their personal preferences.
- If a judgment emerges, the facilitator asks for the evidence on which the judgment is based.

III. Asking questions about the work
- The facilitator asks the group, "What questions does this work raise for you?"
- Group members state any question they have about the work, the child, the assignment, the circumstances under which the work was carried out, and so on.
- The presenting teacher may choose to make notes about these questions, but s/he does not respond to them now – nor is s/he obligated to respond to them in Step V during the time when the teacher speaks.

IV. Speculating about what the student is working on
- The facilitator asks the group, "What do you think the child is working on?"
- Participants, based on their reading or observation of the work, make suggestions about the problems or issues that the student might have been focused on in carrying out the assignment.

Table 5.3 Continued

V. Hearing from the presenting teacher
- The facilitator invites the presenting teacher to speak.
- The presenting teacher provides his or her perspective on the student's work, describing what s/he sees in it, responding (if s/he chooses) to one or more of the questions raised, and adding any other information that s/he feels is important to share with the group.
- The presenting teacher also comments on anything surprising or unexpected that s/he heard during the describing, questioning, and speculating phases.

VI. Discussing implications for teaching and learning
- The facilitator invites everyone (the participants and the presenting teacher) to share any thoughts they have about their own teaching, children's learning, or ways to support this particular child in future instruction.

VII. Reflecting on the CAC
- The group reflects on the experiences of or reactions to the conference as a whole or to particular parts of it.

VIII. Thank the presenting teacher
- The session concludes with acknowledgment of and thanks to the presenting teacher.

Source: Looking at Student Work; http://www.lasw.org/CAC_steps.html

In the late 1980s, Steve Seidel and colleagues at Project Zero developed the Collaborative Assessment Conference protocol. This protocol, like the RTI approach, opens lines of communication among educators in the interest of supporting individual students. The conference was designed to encourage teachers to share questions and hypotheses with colleagues, in order to gain multiple perspectives on pieces of students' work. As a result of the collaboration, teachers leave the conference with a greater understanding than they had prior to the conference session. The following case study illustrates a modified Collaborative Assessment Conference. As you read the case, consider how the child care center director implements the conference with the staff. Think about which moments in the case study provide evidence of the educators' learning, made visible through this description. How was one person's thinking clearly and directly influenced by fellow teachers' comments?

Case Study: Staff Meeting Metamorphosis

Joanie looks at the clock—4:55 p.m. Only five minutes before the monthly staff meeting and she's sweating. Her stomach is doing flip-flops, and yet the scent of the just-delivered pizza fills the room, making her hungry. She closes her eyes and tries to notice her breathing, counting as she breathes in, "1 . . . 2 . . . 3 . . . 4 . . . 5" and exhales, "1 . . . 2 . . . 3 . . . 4 . . . 5." There's a knock at the door, and her assistant director, Carol, peeks in saying, "Are you ready? The gang is all set up, and they're hungry!" Joanie stands up and smoothes out her skirt. "Let's do it!" she says to Carol, as she gives her a "high-five" and then heads down the hall, carrying the pizza boxes. As she walks down the hall she thinks to herself, "Hey—these boxes could always serve as protection if anyone throws something at me!" She smiles, wryly.

***

A month ago Joanie had lost her temper during the staff meeting. She had been tired that evening, finishing the work submitting the center's accreditation application on time, so when the preschool teachers started complaining about all of the tasks they felt were being piled on to them, she'd lost her cool. She yelled at the whole group, chiding them for being so unmotivated and lazy. "No one ever thanks me for making sure that all the toilets flush properly, but that's part of *my* job!" she'd yelled, and slammed down her notebook. Over time, it seemed as if the teachers had been complaining more and more, and the staff meetings had started to feel like a gripe session, instead of being a comfortable time and space for professional growth and reflection.

When she called a close colleague, Sandy, to confess how she'd lost her temper and seek his suggestions for repairing the damage she felt she'd done in terms of her relationships with staff, Sandy told her about a new strategy he'd been using with the teachers at this center. Joanie had been so excited by the time they hung up the phone, that she'd stayed up until almost 2:00 a.m. She had typed up a memo to all of the teachers, outlining a new format for staff meetings, which she presented to them the next morning in their mailboxes, along with a call for volunteers.

***

Joanie had not been surprised that Natalia and Josh were the first two teachers to volunteer to bring in documentation of students' work or play. Joanie knew how closely they worked together, and how strong their communication skills were with each other, with the preK group, and with the families. She'd therefore challenged them by requesting that their documentation be in the form of videotape, and she literally put her money where her mouth was by purchasing an inexpensive hand-held video camera for each classroom. Joanie met with Natalia and Josh a week before the staff meeting, to go over the video footage and the protocol that Sandy had shared with her. The three of them identified a 5-minute video clip of one child, Sam, that they all found compelling, and then made a clear plan for how the flow of the meeting would go, and who would be responsible for each part of the presentation. The structure was planned as follows:

5:00–5:20   Pizza and social time

5:20–5:30   Natalia and Josh present their documentation to the group, and don't speak while the group watches the video clip. The group watches the video clip a second time.

5:30–5:45   Josh asks the group, "What do you notice?" Individual group members then take turns saying something in response to the question.

5:45–6:15   The group watches the video clip a third time, and individuals respond to the question Natalia asks, "What evidence of learning do you see?"

6:15–6:30   Natalia and Josh provide their perspectives on the video clip, elaborating on teachers' ideas and sharing hypotheses they have about specific moments in the clip. They share new ideas and questions that have emerged as a result of the group protocol, and give at least two examples of how this new knowledge will translate into their classroom practice.

***

Throughout the staff meeting, Joanie can't believe how engaged all of the teachers are. Even the preschool teachers keep to the protocol and utter not a single complaint!

Tracy, a Toddler 1 teacher, notices an initial gesture Sam makes in the first minute of the video clip, reaching his hand in the air. J.J., a Toddler 2 teacher, then comments, "It's clear Natalia wants to help Sam achieve his goal. She uses three different strategies to support him." Then J.J. lists the strategies he observed in the video clip. Alex, a preschool teacher, follows the train of thought by adding his opinion about how Sam was encouraged to take an active role in the pursuit of his goals, and his co-teacher Richard notes how both Natalia and Sam shared joy in Sam's success at reaching a sub-goal. Carol is frantically acting as scribe, trying to capture everyone's comments. Joanie makes a mental note about purchasing a digital audio recorder with money from their recent car wash fundraiser.

***

The next morning, Joanie walks into the kitchen to make a fresh pot of coffee for the staff. As she grabs a cold piece of pizza from the fridge for breakfast, she laughs at how nervous she was 24 hours ago. She listens to the buzz of teachers in the halls, getting ready for the morning, and is thrilled to hear them speaking about plans to use the video cameras in their rooms. She's not sure if all future staff meetings will feel as electric as the one last night, but for now, she's excited about the potential, and feels the most director-like she's felt in a long time. She can't wait to call Sandy in a few hours to talk about ways she can capitalize on the staff's enthusiasm and ask for suggestions about how best to share video clips with families on their center's private website.

As teachers who consider the context of children's learning important, the use of authentic assessments that promote collaboration and co-constructed interpretations of children's learning is vital to effective classroom practices. There are different ways to capture the competence of young children in their natural environments, engaging in activities that capture their attention and inspire new investigations. In the next chapter, children's play is discussed as it relates to children's development and education, and also how close examination of children's play provides assessment with integrity.

Summary

Our view of children as curious and capable learners is informed through the use of authentic assessments that produce much information about children's potential. Authentic assessments take many forms, such as portfolios, performance assessments, group assessments and explorations, and self-assessments. The flexibility that authentic assessments afford educators is appealing for many reasons. Teachers can tailor curriculum experiences to provide children with meaningful, real-life experiences that will serve them well as learners, and not simply "regurgitators" of information deemed important by federal and state standards. Combined with standardized assessments, authentic assessment practices contribute to greater opportunities for accurate and efficient interventions with young children than any one assessment practice alone could generate. Authentic assessments place an emphasis on individual children, and tell teachers and families much about children's interests, motivations, and challenges. Through collaborative efforts, supported within a school or district or among teacher colleagues, important implications for classroom instruction and children's future development are identified. Specific strategies, such as Response to Intervention and Looking at Students' Work, are gaining popularity because of the collaborative process and the focus on student-produced products or outcomes.

Now What?

1. The use of authentic assessment carries with it certain responsibilities. What are some considerations that teachers must address when planning authentic assessments that will contribute to advocacy efforts on behalf of individual children?
2. Authentic assessment practices have grown in popularity over several decades in response to the increase of standardized assessments. What are some cautions that the public should be aware of when interpreting data from authentic assessments?
3. After reading this chapter on authentic assessment, how do you feel about these practices and approaches? Select one example or form of authentic assessment presented in the chapter, and show how a stimulating environment can help to promote children's future growth.

Avenues for Inquiry

Looking at Students' Work

This website focuses on Looking at Students' Work, and provides a virtual Collaborative Assessment Protocol that visitors can read and listen to in order to gain a better sense of collaborative assessment that is anchored in students' work. Links to additional resources and research are provided for further exploration.

http://www.lasw.org/CAC_description.html

teachertube.com

The link below takes you to a teachertube.com video clip of a child, Jung Woo, assessing his own reading through a self-assessment. After watching a video of himself reading, he answers questions to evaluate his reading, and then discusses his opinions with his teacher, using examples to support his conclusions. Notice how their conversation is rich with information about Jun Woo's learning, and how the collaboration brings his understanding to a higher level.

http://www.teachertube.com/viewVideo.php?video_id=153379and title=Jung_Woo_reading_self_assessment

Educators for Social Responsibility

This is the website for Educators for Social Responsibility, an organization with the slogan, "creating schools where young people want to be, and teachers want to teach." The site features projects, programing, and resources aimed at cultivating learning environments that are safe and stimulating, and that nurture meaningful relationships among members of the learning community in its broadest sense.

http://esrnational.org

6

The Purpose, Power, and 'Portance of Play

> I recall watching a mother showing her eight-month-old flash cards with pictures of presidents on them. Why it is important for an eight-month-old to learn the names and faces of the presidents, and how one would expect an infant to accomplish this, is beyond my comprehension. Nonetheless, the mother kept at it despite the baby's squirming, which indicated that he had enough. Eventually he threw up, expressing my sentiments exactly.
>
> (Elkind, 2007, p. 93)

David Elkind's sentiments are shared by many parents, teachers, and child advocates who fear that children's time for play is becoming endangered, and potentially extinct in many contexts, such as public classrooms. In the example described above, an exchange between mother and child that had the potential for cuddling and emotional connection was reduced to a "teachable moment." Similar to some features of authentic assessment, play offers children and adults an opportunity to learn and explore. "Play is a process, not a product. We have to learn to trust to the innate wisdom of children and allow them to get on with it . . . play is both doing and becoming. It is in the moment and should be valued as such" (Wilson, 2009, p. 3). While play scenarios may generate products in various forms, those products spring naturally from children's behavior and imagination, and not from the desire of adults to generate data.

One of the main reasons that unstructured free play is disappearing from children's lives is because adults, out of concern for children's academic progress, consider play to be a waste of time. They don't recognize that, for children, "play is not a means to an end, but an end itself" (Kelly-Vance & Ryalls, 2005, p. 549). Adults make judgments about the quality of play based largely on stories in the media or concerns expressed by politicians—some kinds of play are therefore deemed educational, while other kinds of play are considered frivolous. Early childhood educators around the world have noticed a trend in adult assessments of children's play, and argue that "perhaps this misses the very essence of play, which is always an expression of children's subjective experience and thus defies adult representation" (Lester & Russell, 2010, p. 7). If one of the underlying goals of education is to develop human beings, and if play is the leading source of development for young children, then classrooms that provide ample opportunities for play and exploration are providing a great service in the interest of educational goals and our nation's promise.

Play Assessment

A challenge that makes it difficult for many adults to understand or be convinced of the value of play is that it is not something readily quantifiable. Educators and psychologists, for example, have found it difficult to define play behavior. This has been one of the obstacles to developing assessments of play that can be generalized to broad populations and therefore considered valid in the context of education or human development. The fact that much of what experts praise as beneficial about play comes about as the result of observational assessment, and is therefore considered subjective, has resulted in play behavior being difficult to standardize and quantify (Stagnitti, 2004).

In terms of clinical assessment, play often has a complementary role in the assessment of young children. Play as a means of assessment is growing in use among school psychologists, who recognize the benefits of assessment practices in one context (play) that are linked to interventions in the same play context. Therapists use play as a way to gain access to information in a nonintrusive way. While children are engaged in play, therapists gain observational data and insights into other areas of functioning, such as attention, motor skills and sensory processing and integration (Stagnitti, 2004).

The National Association of School Psychologists (NASP) has endorsed the use of play assessment as an "appropriate approach to evaluating the needs of young children" (NASP, 2005). Supporters of this approach to assessment also note that play assessment and related intervention meets the Response to Intervention (RTI) portion of the Individuals with Disabilities Act 2004, to be discussed in Chapter 7. Play assessments typically take various forms, such as direct observations of a child in a natural (non-clinical) setting (e.g. home, classroom, playground), or a child's "play history" gained through parent interview or survey.

Figure 6.1 Hands-on Play

Short-term and Long-term Benefits

Whereas some benefits relating to play assessment, such as interventions that impact children's behavior or cognitive development, are evident within a short period of time (Kelly-Vance & Ryalls, 2005), many benefits of play are long-lasting and less visible in the short-term. Teachers and parents often consider the value of play, such as role playing, preparation for adult roles and situations that children will encounter later in life, which gives play some form of merit when no other argument is available. Yet while child development experts agree that "when children play house, doctor, or police person, they are engaging in activities that will prepare them for taking on adult roles," they clarify that "children are not preparing for life, they are actively living their lives. Children's play takes its meaning from the here and now, not from the future" (Elkind, 2001, p. 28).

If a more serious, scientific argument is needed to convince people of the importance of play, there is evidence from brain science to suggest that the flexibility required for spontaneous, unstructured play serves an evolutionary purpose. The constant change and unpredictability that play affords, as distinct from other activities, serves to promote the brain's "potential for plasticity and openness rather than close down potentiality through rigid and stereotypical behavior" (Lester & Russell, 2010, p.13).

If we strive to provide educational opportunities for children that result in stronger, more creative brains, then we are in sync with children's natural inclinations, providing them with vital resources, as opposed to trying to force them to behave in a scholarly fashion at an age that is simply not appropriate and essentially robs them of their childhood (Carlsson-Paige, 2008).

Historical Views

It is useful to understand how play has been perceived over time, and explained in theory, to argue most effectively in favor of play as healthy for children's development and a legitimate means of assessing their development in childhood. Generally speaking, adults convey a range of attitudes towards children's play: for some, play is simply loud and disruptive; some view play as potentially harmful or immoral; and others consider play as a vehicle for educating children. Around the world, people consider play according to their own cultural standards, but it has been established as an important right for children, and not just a learning tool.

The Right to Play

In 1989, the United Nations Convention on the Rights of the Child (CRC) was convened. Delegates to the convention drafted a document that is cited often in research literature focused on early childhood, particularly children's play. Article 31 contains the following language:

1. States Parties recognize the right of the child to rest and leisure, to engage in play and recreational activities appropriate to the age of the child and to participate freely in cultural life and the arts.
2. States Parties shall respect and promote the right of the child to participate fully in cultural and artistic life and shall encourage the provision of appropriate and equal opportunities for cultural, artistic, recreational, and leisure activity.

                                                                (Lester & Russell, 2010, p. ix)

There is cultural variation that is inextricably linked to countries' unique histories, values, and many other factors, but play as a universal human right that is critical to children's survival is quite powerful. When viewed as a universal human right, it influences how adults encourage and engage in play with children, the influence of gender on play, and the kinds of play that evolve over time.

Children's rights under the CRC are grouped into three categories: survival and development, protection, and participation (for full list see http://www.unicef.org/crc/index_30177.html). Furthermore, providing for children's play is noted as adults' responsibility. When adults provide opportunities and supportive environments, children are empowered and able to create their own play—play that is the primary way in which children enter into their own communities as active members.

Though the value of play has been formally recognized as a result of the CRC, the theoretical history of the role of play in early childhood is what has had the most direct influence on how play is considered in terms of classroom applications and early childhood teacher education.

Theory

The contention that play impacts cognitive development is revolutionary to some people. Through play, children solve complex dilemmas. Play encourages flexible thinking and abstract thought, as well as social skills. School programs that are "play-based" have been shown to have a long-lasting, positive impact on children throughout their lifetimes (Schweinhart et al., 1993). As you read the ideas of the men and women discussed below, in a chronological order, consider how ideas may have influenced the ideas of other thinkers, and how you have seen traces of these theories manifest in early childhood settings.

Froebel

When Friedrich Froebel (1782–1852) wrote and spoke about children's play in the early 1800s, he stated, "Play is the highest expression of what is in the child's soul" (Froebel, 1912, p. 50). Froebel advocated for free play, rather than rote transmission of information. Considered the "father of kindergarten," Froebel thoughtfully designed materials for his children's gardens as a series of 20 "gifts"—hands-on activities that encouraged children to create their own meaning and understanding using a variety of materials. He envisioned that the gifts would develop children's use of the environment as an educational support. He believed that the environment provides children with a sense of connection with nature, and that the materials would nurture and sustain a bond between children and adults who play with them.

Freud

Sigmund Freud (1856–1939) considered early childhood to be the most significant period in terms of the impact that childhood has on later development. Although he did not explicitly discuss play in the context of education, he believed that play provides us with a window into our unconscious. For example, through their play, children often "reveal emotional attachments, fears, or anxieties that they are unable to express in words" (Elkind, 2001, p. 27). The use of play in children's therapy is one way that Freud's ideas are applied in contemporary society, and every early childhood educator can underscore the importance of play for allowing children to express ideas and feelings that might otherwise be unaddressed or repressed.

Piaget

Like Freud, Jean Piaget (1896–1980) believed that children learn through play. He felt that curiosity is the force behind their desire to learn, and that children construct their knowledge through active involvement. Piaget argued that children must be interested in and engaged in learning experiences and saw cooperation as especially important for active learning to occur. Piaget described how engaging in play helps children experience moral dilemmas and conflicts, and to recognize differences in opinions and perspectives. When children's play results in cognitive conflict, the uncomfortable state is called disequilibrium (when new information challenges existing knowledge, beliefs, or assumptions). Piaget also discussed the terms assimilate and accommodate with respect to play's influence on cognitive development. To assimilate means to work new information into an existing way of thinking or belief system, and to accommodate means that a child needs to modify her thinking or beliefs to make sense of new information.

Piaget's developmental stages of play reflect elements of cognitive development found in his proposed stages of cognitive development:

- Sensorimotor play (birth to 2 years): characterized by repetition; children repeat the same activity over and over.
- Symbolic play (2–7): constructive (with materials), dramatic (pretend play where one thing/person represents another), and sociodramatic play (pretend play with other children involving mutual reciprocity).
- Games with rules (7–11): games with clearly defined roles and rules.

A fundamental aspect of play, according to Piaget, is the active, hands-on approach to learning that children love. He believed children need to have a hand in the definition of and transformation of space. This includes considering things from multiple perspectives.

Vygotsky

Like Piaget, Lev Vygotsky (1896–1934) believed that children actively construct their own meaning and knowledge, and play is a primary vehicle for doing so.

Vygotsky proposed that play should be the leading activity for young children. Considering social interactions and communication crucial factors in development, he saw play as an activity involving an imaginary situation created by children. Children explore social roles and rules in their play, and use language to negotiate and develop their understanding.

In today's early childhood classrooms, Vygotsky's ideas can be seen in children's "productive" activities such as storytelling, block building, art and drawing, which occur in a developmentally appropriate social context (Bodrova & Leong, 2007). Teachers use observation to plan hands-on, interactive environments and to scaffold children's learning, and provide opportunities and support for children's collaborative efforts.

Montessori

Italian educator Maria Montessori (1870–1952) coined the phrase "Play is the Child's Work." According to Montessori, there was little value in children's play unless it was put to some practical purpose.

> Freedom without organization of work would be useless. The child left *free* without means of work would go to waste . . . The organization of the work, therefore, is the cornerstone of this new structure of goodness: but even that organization would be in vain without the liberty to make use of it, and without freedom for the expansion of all those energies which spring from the satisfaction of the child's highest activities.
>
> (Montessori, 1965, pp. 188–89)

The notion of children's play as serving an educational purpose, coupled with the attention that the classroom materials designed by Montessori received, prompted the growth of a whole industry called "educational toys" (Elkind, 2001). While educators such as David Elkind recognize that "[l]ove, work, and play are three inborn drives that power human thought and action throughout the life cycle" (Elkind, 2007, p. 3), Elkind distinguishes between work and play, cautioning that they should not be clumped into one category.

Similar to Piaget, Montessori noted what happens when a child learns the meaning of a specific activity, and then begins to enjoy repeating it, "sometimes a seemingly infinite number of times, with the most evident satisfaction. He enjoys executing that act because by means of it he is developing his psychic abilities (Montessori, 1964, p. 357). She also described learning as a constructive process that grows out of a child's innate desire for order. Provided with independence and real working materials, the child becomes conscious of his own powers.

Unlike Vygotsky's emphasis on the social nature of learning, Montessori placed much emphasis on individual learners, not the group. She proposed the role of teacher to be an observer of children, who can provide appropriate guidance about materials and support them when necessary, depending on the individual child. Montessori designed the materials in a standardized progression, to help develop concrete patterns of order in the young child's mind. Montessori's materials reflected Piaget's ideas about children's cognitive development, moving from the more concrete to the abstract (Hainstock, 1986). Although she saw value in children's fantasy play, Montessori felt it important for children to know the difference between fantasy and reality.

Reggio Emilia

An Italian approach to education that is not attributed to one individual, but rather the entire city, the Reggio Emilia approach to early childhood education values play as a fundamental "language" of childhood—a way of expressing and communicating. Loris Malaguzzi (1920–94), considered the founder or "teacher-theorist" of the approach, wrote in his internationally acclaimed poem, *No way. The hundred is there*:

> The child
> is made of one hundred.
> The child has
> a hundred languages
> a hundred hands
> a hundred thoughts
> a hundred ways of thinking
> of playing, of speaking.
> A hundred always a hundred
> ways of listening

of marveling of loving
a hundred joys
for singing and understanding
a hundred worlds
to discover
a hundred worlds
to invent
a hundred worlds
to dream.

(excerpt from poem translated by Lella Gandini,
in Edwards, Gandini, & Forman, 1998)

The children and teachers in Reggio Emilia engage in long-term projects that reflect elements of progressive education. Play, like the projects that often involve play, is valued for its contribution to children's development. The classrooms are places that embody respect for children's curiosity and natural inclinations, where teachers are co-learners and guides, with no pressure to achieve adult-generated benchmarks. Carlina Rinaldi so eloquently writes:

> The dimension of play (with words, playing tricks, and so on) is thus an essential element of the human being. If we take this dimension away from children and from adults, we remove a possibility for learning, we break up the dual play-learning relationship. The creative process, instead, needs to be recognized and legitimated by others.
>
> (Rinaldi, 2006)

In order to define play or consider educational implications for play, it is important to think about various kinds of play that are evident among young children. Table 6.1 presents Bob Hughes' Taxonomy of Play—an extensive list of play categories and related qualities.

Recognizing Significance in Ordinary Moments

Being able to recognize play is only part of the picture. Recognizing the significance in playful activities and arguing for that significance is an important part of responsible teaching and advocating. "Much of play's 'ordinary' action can shift and change direction, in many ways, through its unpredictable and dynamic nature. Yet at the same time, through the very process of playing, it can make critical differences to a child's experience of time and space" (Lester & Russell, 2010, p. 10).

One of the biggest advocates for children and children's play, educator and author Vivian Paley, recognizes the influence that play has on a child's

Table 6.1 Hughes's Taxonomy of Play

Symbolic play: when a stick becomes a horse

Rough and tumble play: play fighting

Socio-dramatic play: social drama

Social play: playing with rules and societal structures

Creative play: construction and creation

Communications play: words, jokes, acting, body and sign languages, facial expressions

Dramatic play: performing or playing with situations that are not personal or domestic, (e.g. playing "Harry Potter" or doing a "Harry Potter" play)

Deep play: risky experiences that confront fear

Exploratory play: manipulating, experimenting

Fantasy play: rearranges the world in the child's fantastical way

Imaginative play: pretending

Locomotor play: chase, swinging, climbing, playing with the movements of your body

Mastery play: lighting fires, digging holes, games of elemental control

Object play: playing with objects and exploring their uses and potential

Recapitulative play: carrying forward the evolutionary deeds of becoming a human being (e.g. dressing up with paints and masks, damming streams, growing food)

Role play: exploring other ways of being, pretending to drive a bus or be a policeman or use a telephone

---

Source: Wilson, P. (2009).

lifelong development. She has dedicated her career to making evident the wonder and power inherent in children's everyday, ordinary play.

The Work and Wisdom of Vivian Paley

Drawing upon her years teaching kindergarten, Paley acknowledges that "[k]indergarteners are passionate seekers of hidden identities and quickly respond to those who keep unraveling the endless possibilities" (Paley, 1997, p. 4). In the quotes that follow, taken from her 1997 book, *The girl with the brown crayon,* you can see how Paley draws the reader into her experiences witnessing the genius of young children's thinking that results from free play. In one example, Paley notes children's considerations of philosophy and the arts, stating, "In the course of a morning, the children have taken up such matters as the artist's role in society, the conditions necessary for thinking, and the influence of music and art on the emotions" (p. 8). In another description, Paley admires Reeny's observation and empathy, writing, "Reeny admires Oliver. She was the first to copy his rabbits, even before she fell in love with Leo Lionni's mice. It was she who noticed that Oliver uses one color to a page and will not answer questions that begin with 'why'" (p. 27). When children are given time and materials to make their own connections, and when a skilled teacher documents children's play, it is easy for outsiders—readers—to draw conclusions based on evidence. Throughout the book, Paley analyzes children with an anthropologist's eye and a philosopher's sensibility.

It is during children's play that children often change and transform their roles, objects, and themes. This type of flexible thinking has been linked to creativity, which supports Piaget's ideas about play being a means by which children construct knowledge. Specifically, logico-mathematical knowledge is developed through the act of associating, classifying, and sorting materials (Bergen, 2009).

It is sometimes challenging for educators to convey the importance of play on children's thinking, and how it lays the groundwork for math, literacy, science, and other content knowledge. Bergen (2009) notes, "young children often demonstrate interest in mathematical concepts in their play and this interest is usually fostered by preschool teachers. When these children enter kindergarten, however, their interests may not be encouraged by a standardized curriculum" (Bergen, 2009, citing Assouline & Lupkowski-Shoplik, 2005, p. 262). In the case study that follows, you will read about an experience in which unstructured play on the part of one student led to extensions of play and enhancements in teaching as a result of free, lightly structured play.

Case Study: A Ball Turns into a Sculpture

"Taylor, where is your project?" Mary asks, as she notices Taylor twirling around the pole in the middle of the classroom for the third or fourth time. Five-year-old Taylor doesn't appear to pay any attention, and Mary sighs. It's been a long week. She sits down on the stool nearest her and places her hand on Taylor's ball of clay. "Taylor—please come get your clay before we call it a day," she calls to him, deciding that she's not going to make a big deal out of the twirling. "Pick your battles, pick your battles" she repeats silently to herself, and walks over to him.

Mary puts her hand on Taylor's shoulder gently and offers the ball of clay to him—"Here's your project. If you wrap it in a wet paper towel it should still be soft enough for next time." Taylor looks at the clay, and at Mary, with a blank expression on his face. As Mary turns to walk back to the table, she sees Taylor throw his ball of clay on the floor. One of Taylor's classmates, Yazmin, calls out, "Whoa! Look what happened to Taylor's ball! It changed shape!" Her eyes are wide with excitement. Eli comes over to take a look at Taylor's ball, now a slanted blob, and throws his own ball of clay on the floor. A ripple of enthusiasm erupts across the room.

***

On any other day, Mary might have stepped in to stop this behavior, but today she decides to see what happens. Sitting on the stool, she calls out encouragement to the children in her small group as they experiment with throwing balls of clay. Eli throws a smaller ball and squeals, "It bounced! That's cool!" Aisha stands on the rungs of a stool to get a better view, and Mary calls to her, "Aisha—what would happen if you throw a ball down from up there?" Aisha shrugs her shoulders up to her ears and giggles. She raises her hand, palm down, holding the ball of clay up over her head, waits a few seconds, and then drops it—plunk! After a few minutes of playing with throwing the balls of clay, the children's action slows to a stop as they begin noticing the effects of their experimentation. Mary asks the group, "What happens when the balls are thrown on the floor?" Several children respond:

"It has a flat side and a bumpy side!"

"It looks like a bunch of mountains or a beehive."

"It gets squished. It gets flat."

"Somebody stepped on one and now it has shoe prints and bumps."

Mary notices Isabella sitting quietly to the side, and asks, "What do you think, Isabella?" Isabella pauses for a moment, then says matter-of-factly, "We should make a book about it." Mary takes her digital camera out of her work bag and hands it to Isabella, who leaps up and starts photographing the clay balls on the floor.

At the end of the day, when the whole group is together for circle time, Mary shows the class some pictures of the small group's play, throwing the clay balls. She asks the children, "What do the balls of clay remind you of?"

Yazmin says, "It looks like sand squished into cookies."

Eli says, "Like lots of little cookies."

Aisha offers, "It reminds me of lily pads!"

Taylor says, "It looks like clay thrown on the floor."

Several of the children ask if they can fire the clay balls, so the whole class goes through the arduous process of getting the clay off of the floor. Some of the clay balls are hard to lift off, and some stretch and break, but they are able to lift many pieces off the floor and they place these pieces on the greenware tray, where they will be transferred to the kiln for bisque firing over the weekend.

***

On Monday afternoon, Mary brings the small group over to the round table in the back of the classroom, and shows them all of the pieces of recently fired clay. She asks the group, "What should we do with all of these pieces?" Aisha's hand shoots up as she exclaims, "Let's make a sculpture!" After the rest of the students nod and comment in agreement, they grab jars of glaze and begin to paint the pieces. Isabella resumes her photography, walking around the room to take pictures of the students and their painting.

***

Two days later, Mary once again brings the small group to the round table and reaches under the table, producing a large cardboard box. As she places the box on the tabletop, the clay pieces inside clink together, making distinctive sounds. Eli peeks inside the box and says, "It's shiny now after it was fired and the color changed when it got cooked!" This leads the group into a discussion about the glaze firing process. Yazmin notices, "It feels like metal. It sounds like metal." Taylor says, "It has different colors now. They turned different colors than the paint was." His eyebrows are furrowed as he examines a piece of clay closely.

Isabella continues to take photos of the group during discussion, and Mary asks the students, "So you want to make a sculpture, right? What should we do? What kind of sculpture do you want to make?" Some children want to create individual sculptures, and others want the whole class to work together. Aisha suggests a new idea—"We could use the pieces of clay to write our names?" This idea seems to excite the students, until they discover that there aren't enough pieces for everyone to write their names.

Isabella exclaims, "We still aren't working together!" and frowns.

Eli says, "What if we worked together to write one word?"

Taylor responds, "What if we can't spell it yet?"

Isabella offers, "We can write 'art.'"

Aisha says, "Let's sound it out," and Isabella says, "I'll take the pictures."

***

Aisha writes the word "art" on a piece of paper and hangs it on the wall for everyone to see. Together, the children form the word using pieces of fired clay.

Eli says, "Now let's write the word 'together!'"

Taylor replies, "That's a really long word."

Isabella suggests, "We can do it together."

Aisha proudly says, "I already know how to spell it: T-O-G-E-T-H-E-R!"

***

At the end of the month, as Mary prepares her family newsletter, she looks at photos that Isabella took during the clay experience. Smiling as she remembers the excitement that captured the children's interest during that week, she decides to create a visual essay to go in the newsletter. As she places the photos using her "publisher" software, she's inspired to create a new feature in the newsletter, linking the children's play to standards so that parents will have a better understanding of how play is also a vehicle for children's learning. Mary chooses two examples from the kindergarten science, technology, and engineering standards:

Physics is the study of matter . . . It deals with speed, leverage, balance, gravity, and mechanical systems. Young children can grasp these concepts through exploratory play.

Chemistry deals with . . . transformations of substances . . . Through cooking, mixing, and art experiences, children can observe how chemical transformations take place through heat, moisture, and combining substances.

"Thank goodness I was tired that day!" Mary thinks to herself, and looks over at Taylor in the reading area. "Hey, Taylor!" she calls to him. He looks up from his book, and Mary smiles, saying, "Nice work!"

As a result of the clay ball experiences, Taylor gained entry into the class's activities, and established expertise that children can use in their own work, and reference for others. The social benefits that accompany ordinary play activities are as valuable, if not more so, than cognitive gains. As children strive to make sense of their world, and all of its complications, play provides an avenue for sense-making, and provides teachers with fodder for stimulating activities that enhance development.

Social and Emotional Competence

It has been suggested that active learning is important for children's development. In early childhood classrooms, play is best supported in a nexus of secure, consistent relationships (Bullard, 2010). Research in the field of brain science suggests that helping children interact with their current physical and social environments has both physical and cognitive benefits (Lester & Russell, 2010, p. x). If teachers can build strong arguments about the merits of social interactions for cognitive development, then many parents would view play as less frivolous and more important for future academic success.

Bumps and Bruises

Children's social and emotional competence is desired for all children, and challenging for teachers and parents to guide in a society that seems to focus on violence and fighting more than altruistic behaviors. This prompts many teachers to discourage, even avoid, children's play during school. In place of unstructured play, some teachers design other activities that feel easier to manage and perhaps have an educational, therefore productive agenda. "Reducing playtime may seem in the short term to reduce problems, but this approach does not address the wide-ranging needs children address through play" (Levin, 2003). Furthermore, consistent reduction in or elimination of play has a negative impact on children's emotion-regulation systems, which affects their physical, social, and cognitive competence (Pellis & Pellis, 2006).

Using simple observation skills, teachers and parents can observe the types of play that children participate in, and can work toward establishing classroom and home environments that support their play and curriculum. Table 6.2 features Parten's descriptions of play, which have been used for decades to provide a framework for identifying and discussing children's play. Play that might appear on the surface to be physical or violent is often benign, and developmentally appropriate. It is often the most scary or confusing content that children struggle to work out and understand, and often those who have little access to emotional and physical resources need the outlet the most (Levin, 2003).

Similar to the way adults can't define play from the same perspective as children, adults also should not interpret play through their own adult lenses without considering the child's perspective. The violence that children might incorporate in their dramatic play is not weighed with the same cognitive and moral scales that adults possess. Children strive to feel powerful and competent during many stages of life, and play is one way they achieve mastery over content and physical challenges.

Assessment of children's play opens channels for discussion about issues such as violence and fearful things, but also cultural expectations

Table 6.2 Parten's Social Descriptions of Play

Unoccupied: uninvolved in play.

Onlooker: the child watches others play and may ask questions.

Solitary: the child plays alone not interacting with others.

Parallel: the child plays near others. She may mirror the play of the other child but typically does not engage in conversation.

Associative: the child begins to play with other children.

Cooperative: the child plays in a group. This play is characterized by shared, defined goals.

Source: Parten (1932).

for gender, race, and class. Children are able to test and refute these cultural norms as they structure and challenge boundaries in their play (Wohlwend, 2005). When children are given control over their environment, they can learn to be comfortable with uncertainty and ambiguity and to take moderate risks—two elements that contribute to creativity.

When children are able to take risks during play, they experience the triumphs of success as well as pitfalls and disappointment, but the stakes are not so great—it is a game whose outcome does not have life-threatening consequences, only disequilibrium and temporary discomfort. Children experience joys and positive associations as they encounter elements they previously feared and avoided. Children might never learn to walk, ride a bike, or climb up a knotted rope unless they were intrinsically motivated to take risks despite potential for injury. Children with disabilities and children with little to no access to play spaces have an even greater need for risk-taking opportunities, since they do not have

Figure 6.2
Playing with Fire

immediate access to the safe, collaborative play environments and experiences available to other children. This translates directly into a connection with assessment, in terms of performance on standardized tests, because children are often afraid to take risks when a classroom culture teaches them that getting the wrong answer is bad, and equals failure.

The Play Imperative

Experts in the field of early childhood education and child development argue strongly that the reduction in children's play poses "dire consequences—not only for children but for the future of our nation" (Miller & Almon, 2009, p. 1). The report, *Crisis in the kindergarten: why children need to play in school*, was published by the Alliance for Childhood, an organization dedicated to improving children's lives through policy change and advocacy efforts. The authors received worldwide response and acclaim for the report, which generated much discussion on local and policy levels. Other educators echo the sentiment, calling for a radical reassessment of what is best for children in public education, and changes such as requiring 50 percent of preschoolers' school time for play (Mardell et al., 2010). Recognizing play as a vehicle for fun *and* as a means of learning shifts expectations for adults who might resist the increased attention on play.

Last Child in the Woods

In his book, *Last child in the woods* (2005), author Richard Louv argues that children are experiencing a "nature-deficit disorder." As school administrators reduce the amount of class time dedicated to creative pursuits in the arts, even more school districts fail to offer "hands-on experiences with nature outside the classroom" (Louv, 2005, p. 137).

Louv argues that increasing amounts of technology are part of the problem, but not the main problem, arguing that the "problem with computers isn't computers—they're just tools; the problem is that over-dependence on them displaces other sources of education, from the arts to nature" (p.136).

If yet another nature-based argument is needed to support the benefits of play on children's development, brain science once again suggests how play is a good thing. Taking a cue from animal researchers, who have shown that animals that play the most experience the largest brain growth

Figure 6.3 Leaf Toss

in proportion to their bodies, "[i]t is easy to imagine that similar growth happens in human beings. But it is also easy to imagine what happens to children who do not have this experience in their lives" (Wilson, 2009, p. 4). Children's play is not distinct from other aspects of their lives, and is woven into their work, school, and other daily routines (Punch, 2003).

A Revised Agenda

Although children are smart and crafty enough to find ways of working play into even the most mundane classroom experiences, "the prioritization of adult agendas in political and economic processes can often ride roughshod over children's ability to exercise their right to play, both in everyday life and in extreme circumstances" (Lester & Russell, 2010, p. 2). Until adults—policymakers—come to value and reward play because of its benefits for children's development and the information it provides in terms of assessing children's growth over time, then our nation, and the broader global society, is in danger. "The disappearance of play is especially unfortunate because it is happening at the very time that professionals in many scientific, mathematical, and engineering fields articulate the need for creative and innovative thinkers in their professions" (ibid., p. 414). If educators and legislators wish to produce a new generation of creative problem-solvers, then play is indeed imperative.

> In an era of standardized curriculum and high-stakes testing, educators often find it difficult to take the long view about the qualities of mind they need to develop in potential computer scientists, mathematicians, chemists, physicists, and engineers. In truth, job requirements of many creative and innovative professionals make it especially important for educators to promote such abilities and to realize how the medium of play enhances their development. That makes the disregard of the value of play for mathematics and scientific learning prevalent in most of today's schools especially problematic.
>
> (Bergen, 2009, p. 425)

When children's play is considered valuable in terms of assessment, and a means of assessment that can be conducted in children's natural play environments (e.g. home, school), it is motivating, empowering, and "elicits the highest level of a child's functioning" (Kelly-Vance & Ryalls, 2005, p. 557). Play becomes a natural means for exploring and understanding children's individual differences, which is the focus of the next chapter.

Summary

Although many experts cite the importance of play on children's physical, cognitive, and social development, classrooms are currently places in which play is underemphasized or ignored. For many reasons, such as pressures for accountability, fear about violent or dangerous themes creeping into play, and adults' discomfort with play materials, children are experiencing fewer opportunities for risk-taking, creative exploration, and connections to nature. For over 200 years, educators, philosophers, and psychologists have investigated play and its benefits for children's growth, and the ideas of the day have been translated into classroom environments. As teachers begin to recognize the power of children's ordinary experiences, they will more easily engage and reassure families who worry about their children's competence. When play is viewed through the child development lens, supported by brain science, the argument is strong and sound, and children's individuality is celebrated.

Now What?

1. As you can tell from the material presented in this chapter, experts consider play to be vital for human development and for our nation's successful growth. If you were a parent of a child between 3 and 8 years old, how could you encourage him to go outside and play, and to take moderate risks in his daily play experiences?

2. Given today's pressures for children to demonstrate academic progress, how are children more or less confused about their own power and creativity?

3. Think back to your own childhood. How would you describe your typical play experiences? Do you think your play affected your current behavior? Explain your answer by linking your childhood examples to later personal or professional experiences.

Avenues for Inquiry

Empowered by Play

Empowered by Play supports "imaginative play in our way-too-busy, consumer-driven, media-filled world." This website provides information for families and teachers who wish to protect and promote the precious time of life that is early childhood, and to connect people who share similar hopes for children and their play.

   http://www.empoweredbyplay.org/

Campaign for a Commercial-free Childhood

This website aims to inform and energize parents and teachers in an effort to reduce the influence that businesses and commercial products have on children's lives, particularly play. Many articles about the organizations efforts relating to policy are highlighted, as well as resources to encourage communication and education.

   http://commercialfreechildhood.org/

Old-fashioned Play Builds Serious Skills

This link brings visitors to the National Public Radio website, where a feature story titled *Old-fashioned play builds serious skills* is presented. The site also has an audio recording available—an interview with three child development experts about what is happening to play in public schools. Links to additional resources are available.

   http://www.npr.org/templates/story/story.php?storyId=19212514

7

Vive la Différence

> If teachers don't question the culture and values being promoted in the classroom, they socialize their students to accept the uneven power relations of our society along lines of race, class, gender, and ability. Yet teachers can— and should—challenge the values of white privilege and instead promote values of self-love.
>
> (Segura-Mora, 2008, p. 3)

We live in a diverse society. The power dynamic that is referenced in the above quote research exists. Although educators would like to believe that a respectful classroom is accessible to all children and families, this is not an easy feat, "because, at least in the human development/education fields, we've been taught a deficit model where intellectual, family, and mental health practices that differ from the mainstream, middle-class norm are not viewed as cultural differences but as defects or inadequacies" (Gonzalez-Mena, 2008, p. 13).

Our country perpetuates a great irony, holding up as ideal the notion of cultural pluralism throughout history, yet routinely discriminating against those who don't fit into a standard mold as determined by the majority group. In a real culturally pluralistic society, groups and individuals would "be allowed, even encouraged, to hold on to what gives them their unique identities while maintaining their membership in the larger social framework" (p. 13). Yet in many American schools and classrooms—places where the term "melting pot" still echoes in the hallways, especially around Thanksgiving—children who are deemed "different" do not necessarily feel welcome and valued as contributing members of the broader group.

What makes a child different? For the purposes of this chapter, differences will be discussed in terms of culture and diversity, and classroom applications and practices. As educators and advocates for young children, it is important to recognize the challenges that are linked to differences, and how those differences impact assessment. Recognizing that one chapter in one book presents limitations as to what and how much material is covered, this chapter is intended to provide some basic foundational information and raise some key issues and provocations for continued discussion.

At the most basic level, early childhood educators tend to agree that all children need to feel that they (and their families) are welcome in their classrooms, and respected by their teachers and peers. In order to feel valuable and validated, they need to see themselves reflected in materials throughout the classroom. Materials can include wall decorations, children's books, toys and games, and music.

The National Association for the Education of Young Children (NAEYC) defines culture as including "ethnicity, racial identity, economic class, family structure, language, and religious and political beliefs, which profoundly influence each child's development and relationship to the world" (NAEYC, 2003, p. 2). Put even more simply, culture refers to how people live on a daily basis. This includes "the language we speak, the religion or spirituality we practice (or not), and the clothing, housing, food, and ritual/holidays with which we feel most comfortable" (Derman-Sparks & Edwards, 2010, p. 55). To young children, their family culture is not noticeable—it just is. Piaget's notion of disequilibrium applies to situations when one's culture and assumptions are challenged and therefore cause children or adults to change their thinking to accommodate the new information. As children enter and participate in classroom settings, their awareness of "difference" with respect to culture, and many other factors, develops.

Facets of Diversity

In terms of children's development, consideration of factors that contribute to the child's "context" at a given point of time and over time is important. For children, contextual factors include home, school, and community, but also broader influences such as culture (Bronfenbrenner, 1979). Acknowledging the increasingly diverse society that children are being born into means that we must address contextual inequities that are related to diversity.

Educators have noted that assessment practices in early childhood classroom settings, including public schools, do not always match the influences of children's family culture and language, or developmental abilities. "In an increasingly diverse society, interpretations of assessment results may fail to take into account the unique cultural aspects of children's learning and relationships . . . causing teachers to narrow their curriculum and teaching practices . . . especially when the stakes are high" (NAEYC, 2003, p. 4). In an ideal situation, culturally responsive teachers, curricula, and assessment would support children's diversity, but the reality of pressures to produce evidence of annual yearly progress means that children's learning styles, language, temperaments, and identities are viewed as potential obstacles to successful assessment scores and ratings.

While some discomfort or cognitive conflict of the sort Piaget described actually promotes cognitive development, and stepping out of comfort zones is actually productive and helpful, it is another thing to be uncomfortable on a daily basis because of being forced out of a comfort zone. The term transformative education—when two people or groups come together and interact in such a way that both are transformed—reminds us that cognitive discomfort can be beneficial for children and families. In transformative education roles aren't as important as respectful interactions and ongoing dialogues. When individuals recognize that our individual and collective experiences are important, and when different points of view are respected, transformative education can bring children to new levels of awareness of diversity (Gonzalez-Mena, 2008).

Figure 7.1 illustrates many different family structures. Family structure is but one way in which children are different from each other.

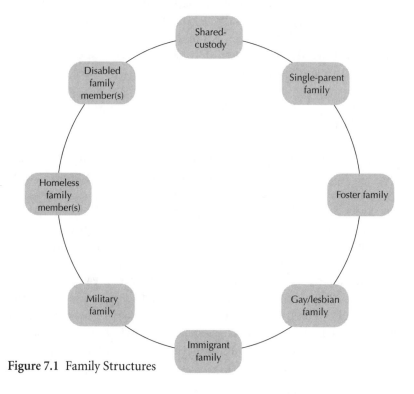

Figure 7.1 Family Structures

Early childhood educational settings that respect and recognize the whole child incorporate curricula that address all aspects of young children's development. This means a focus on social and emotional skills as well as literacy and math skills, and children's physical health in general. Settings that recognize strengths in diversity actively collaborate with families, often providing extended services for families as needed or desired (Espinosa, 2010). Specific federal legislation has been developed over several decades, with respect to two distinct groups of individuals that often require extended services to succeed in mainstream classrooms—children with disabilities and children for whom English is not their native language.

Children with Disabilities

On November 29, 1975, Congress enacted the *Education for All Handicapped Children Act* (Public Law 94-142). This law required public schools accepting federal funds to provide equal access to education for children with physical and mental disabilities, and was designed to guarantee rights for students with disabilities. In 1990, the public law developed into the *Individuals with Disabilities Education Act (IDEA)*, and was amended in 1997. Most recently, George W. Bush and Congress reauthorized the law as the *Individuals with Disabilities Education Improvement Act (IDEA) of 2004.* Individual states are able to establish their own goals for the performance of children with disabilities that are aligned with each state's definition of "annual yearly progress" aligned with *NCLB 2001.* The *IDEA* governs how states and public agencies provide early intervention, special education and other services to more than 6.5 million eligible infants, toddlers, children and youths with disabilities. Under this law, all children with disabilities are entitled to a free appropriate education in the least restrictive environment, and some are entitled to early intervention and other services. Federal oversight of the *IDEA* occurs in the Office of Special Education (OSEP), part of the United States Department of Education. Some key terms related to the mandates for services that the *IDEA* describes are the individualized education program and the least restrictive environment.

Least Restrictive Environment

Students are to remain in their regular classroom, home, and family as much as possible. Their learning environment should be as similar as possible to that of children who do not have a disability. This is also known as inclusion.

Individualized Education Plan (IEP)

A written document (similar to a contract) that details an educational plan for a child to succeed under the supervision and guidance from the family, teachers and professionals, and administrators. The federal government requires schools to assess and diagnose children between ages of 3 and 21 to identify specific learning disabilities. Schools must provide children with thorough educational evaluations to determine whether they need special education services. These evaluations should be sensitive to distinctive learning and developmental factors, such as potential benefits of environmental factors such as online versus paper-and-pencil testing (Kim & Huynh, 2010). Secretary of Education Spellings said, "The days when we looked past the underachievement of these students are over. *No Child Left Behind* and the *IDEA 2004* have not only removed the final barrier separating special education from general education, they also have put the needs of students with disabilities front and center" (Salvia, Ysseldyke, & Bolt, 2009).

Limited English Proficient (LEP)

Because of the close scrutiny associated with standardized assessments and screening, federal regulations also specify when a child shouldn't be identified as learning disabled, specifically if the "discrepancy between ability and achievement is primarily the result of environmental, cultural, or economic disadvantage" (US Department of Education, 1977, p. 65083). The terminology often varies, and children who do not speak English as their native language and encounter educational challenges are referred to as English Language Learners (ELLs) or Limited English Proficient, among other terms. The federal definition of LEP is someone who:

> Has sufficient difficulty speaking, reading, writing, or understanding the English language and whose difficulties may deny such individual the opportunity to learn successfully in classrooms where the language of instruction is English or to participate fully in our society due to one or more of the following reasons:
> 1. was not born in the United States or whose native language is a language other than English and comes from an environment where a language other than English is dominant;

2. is a Native American or Alaska Native or who is a native resident of the Outlying Areas and comes from an environment where a language other than English has had significant impact on such individual's level of English language proficiency; or

3. is migratory and whose native language is other than English and comes from an environment where a language other than English is dominant.

(US Department of Education, 1994)

Given this framework, individual states are left to create their own operational definitions of LEP, which means they also determine methods to identify LEP students. Examples of methods include: student records, teacher observations, teacher interviews, referrals, parent information, children's report cards, home language surveys, informal assessments, and language proficiency/standardized tests. There are practical considerations in identifying children as LEP, such as the variations that exist in children's degrees of proficiency across both their first (native) and their second language, English. It is helpful to consider children's English proficiency along a continuum, as opposed to clear-cut extremes. The following categories are used to describe children's specific language abilities.

Sequential Bilingualism

A person in this category is monolingual and then is exposed to an additional language at a later time. An example of this would be a child born in France, whose family relocates to the United States. The child would learn French first, as a natural language acquisition process, and then would learn English as a result of moving to the US.

Simultaneous Bilingualism

Children in this category typically come from a home where two languages are spoken. Another possibility is when a child is exposed to two languages at the same time from an early age and the child therefore learns both languages at the same time. An example of this could be an English-speaking family hiring a Brazilian nanny. The child would be in the care of both the family and the nanny, and would be exposed to both English and Portuguese.

Elective Bilingualism

This category refers to children whose families speak one language at home, and the children's parents opt to have their child learn a second language. This is common when communities have schools that offer bilingual instruction in specific languages, and parents can request placement in those schools.

Circumstantial Bilingualism

Sometimes specific circumstances force families to learn another language to survive. In these situations the family's native language isn't the dominant language spoken, nor does it have prestige in the community.

When selecting assessments for children whose home language is not English, it is useful to consider the specific categories above and appropriate strategies to use so that children have the best chances for success on the assessments. Of course, additional questions arise, such as whether the assessment instruments are available in the primary language(s) of the children who are to be assessed. The NAEYC position statement on the assessment of young children states:

> For young bilingual children, instructionally embedded assessments using observational methods and samples of children's performance can provide a much fuller and more accurate picture of children's abilities than other methods. Individually, culturally, and linguistically appropriate assessment of all children's strengths, developmental status, progress, and needs provides essential information to early childhood professionals as they attempt to promote children's development and learning.
>
> (NAEYC, 2003, p. 10)

Assessments that are inappropriate because of cultural factors, language, or lack of fit with a child's abilities may not provide an accurate measure of children's intellectual capacities or performance. Numerous factors have the potential to influence a child's performance, such as anxiety about assessment, ambiguous instructions, nutrition, and culturally learned behavior about relating to adults. All of these factors, and combinations of these and others, contribute to the creation of a gap between a particular performance and a child's actual ability. This can result in inaccurate conclusions and recommendations for intervention that can hinder a child's future opportunities.

Mindful teaching and assessment practices with diverse populations of children, coupled with an appreciation for differences that is promoted within a classroom, are components of anti-bias curriculum and instruction.

Anti-bias Curriculum

"In an anti-bias classroom, children learn to be proud of themselves and of their families, to respect human differences, to recognize bias, and to speak up for what is right" (Derman-Sparks & Edwards, 2010, p. 1). Teachers who teach in an anti-bias environment attempt to recognize situations that are potentially damaging to children's senses of self, and teachers develop skills in intervention. For example, immediate intervention (e.g. conversation) and follow-up activities are learned to counter the potentially harmful impact of confusing, hurtful exchanges.

Anti-bias educators take a stance in their work about positive future educational opportunities for their students. Teachers are committed to the idea that every child deserves opportunities to develop to the best of his or her potential. This can be challenging because the tensions between those situated in a position of privilege and those in a position of disadvantage are deeply rooted in American history, as well as the history of other cultural and ethnic groups. Unequal access to resources, and the biases that perpetuate inequity, have an enormous impact on children's lives.

Children's Needs

Because early childhood educators know that children are born ready to learn, they also know children are therefore susceptible to learning prejudice and discrimination at an early age. Some educators are concerned that children are too young to understand the concepts associated with bias. Arguably, since biases begin to affect children's development early, it is developmentally appropriate to include discussions of them in early childhood settings. With thoughtful guidance, children can participate in and appreciate discussions and problem-solving. Young children "need caring adults to help them construct a positive sense of self and a respectful understanding of others" (Derman-Sparks & Edwards, 2010, p. 11). Anti-bias educators stress that it is vital that children begin to know and like who they are without feeling superior to others. Thus, the goals that anti-bias education (ABE) educators focus on aim to foster development of the whole child. Table 7.1 outlines the four core goals of anti-bias education.

Table 7.1 The Four Core Goals of Anti-Bias Education

ABE Goal 1
Each child will demonstrate self-awareness, confidence, family pride, and positive social identities.

ABE Goal 2
Each child will express comfort and joy with human diversity; accurate language for human differences; and deep, caring human connections.

ABE Goal 3
Each child will increasingly recognize unfairness, have language to describe unfairness, and understand that unfairness hurts.

ABE Goal 4
Each child will demonstrate empowerment and the skills to act, with others or alone, against prejudice and/or discriminatory actions.

Source: Derman-Parks & Edwards (2010, p. xiv).

Each of the four anti-bias education goals is dependent on each of the others, and contributes to a better, more successful classroom environment. ABE has at its heart the established relationships among staff and between staff and families. Educators often find it more uncomfortable and frightening to raise issues of diversity and inequity with adults than with children. When adults welcome participation and collaboration, educators feel that they have the benefit of providing more effective anti-bias education for the children and a richer, more complex, and more effective experience for the adults.

Anti-bias work provides teachers with a way to examine and transform their own understanding of children's lives and also do self-reflective work to more deeply understand their own lives and approaches to teaching.

Teachers' Role

In the anti-bias education approach, teachers are encouraged to develop confidence in their own abilities to act in the interest of social justice, which means that they have a strong understanding of their own biases, identity, and cultural beliefs (Chen, Nimmo, & Fraser, 2009). Teachers work to nurture dispositions that will enable them to apply the cultural knowledge and implementation skills they have acquired. Through this lens, teachers learn to see their students' cultures not as obstacles to learning but rather as a means by which students can learn "the official knowledge and skills of the school community" (Ladson-Billings, 2001, p. 99).

Recognizing the benefits of reflective practice, educators Chen, Nimmo, and Fraser (2009) created a tool for beginning teachers. This tool is intended to guide critical self-reflection for teachers at an individual level, and could be useful for novice and veteran teachers. There are four goals embedded in the tool. The first is to raise self-awareness (beliefs and biases that influence personal and professional practices); the second is consideration of the physical environment (selection and use of materials in the classroom); the third is the pedagogical environment (messages conveyed to learners through choice of language, curriculum, teacher's conscious and unconscious strategies); and fourth is the teacher's relationships with families and community settings. Table 7.2 presents elements included in the self-study tool.

As new and seasoned teachers delve into anti-bias work with their students, it is especially useful for them to consider finding a colleague with whom to share the experiences. Teachers so often work in isolation, within the walls of their own classroom environments. Shifting to more

Table 7.2 Sample Self-Study Guide Layout: Raising Self-Awareness–Taking a Look Within

	Not yet: This is new territory for me/Not applicable to my age group.	Sometimes: I have a beginning awareness.	Usually: But I still require conscious effort.	Consistently: I do this with ease.	The next steps for me: My goal is . . .
Am I aware of my own cultural identity and history? How comfortable am I about who I am?					
Am I aware of biases I may hold?					
Do I view diversity and exceptionality as strengths and that ALL children can succeed?					

Adapted from: Chen, Nimmo, & Fraser (2009).

collaborative work is an incredibly refreshing change of pace—teachers need colleagues who support and join with them. Having someone to share ideas and questions with makes the journey richer and helps teachers persist in the face of obstacles. Collaboration also provides multiple perspectives and noticings that might otherwise go unacknowledged. Technology affords many opportunities for collaboration that didn't exist as recently as ten years ago. Blogs, wikis, photo sharing sites, and email provide instant avenues for communication and access to supportive, sensitive colleagues.

Culturally Sensitive Practice

Culturally sensitive practice entails purposeful consideration of the cultural, linguistic, and socio-economic factors that have potential influences on students' classroom success. The premise is that teachers and school personnel become sensitive to cultural and linguistic variations within the community, and incorporate school-wide responsive practices. Attention to cultural and linguistic factors, and the incorporation of these elements in curriculum development, implementation, and assessment will help shape and strengthen connections between the school culture and school-based expectations, and the cultural elements that students bring to the school. Instruction that is differentiated according to students' learning styles and motivations builds on existing student knowledge and experience, and should be language appropriate (NCRTI, 2010).

This may seem like a tall order in an early childhood classroom. Yet honoring cultural differences doesn't mean that teachers must adjust or tailor their philosophies and practices for every single family. It does, however, mean that responsive teachers make an effort to understand specific aspects of cultures so that children and families feel welcome and respected in the classroom and school. Particularly when families speak a different language than the teacher, people tend to rely on nonverbal communication to connect on a personal level. Although not limited to nonverbal exchanges, nonverbal communication can sometimes lead to miscommunication, due to people's unfamiliarity with cultural specifics. The items below are some examples of ways humans interact through nonverbal means, and these are often linked to the senses. Awareness of these is helpful for educators and others who wish to support a culturally sensitive classroom environment.

Personal Space/Closeness

In white-Anglo or European-American interactions, people typically feel most comfortable when they keep themselves at an arm's length from others, such as during conversations. When people from other cultural backgrounds come within the boundaries of someone's personal "bubble," it often can be perceived as hostile or invasive instead of friendly. For example, some young children are huggers, and others are not. It is important to discuss this and to understand that when a 3-year-old hugs a friend with a forceful embrace, it is not necessarily a show of aggression.

Smiling

Some cultural and ethnic groups smile when they are happy, and not necessarily as an invitation to enter into friendship or friendly conversation. Some people perceive big or broad smiles as phony and insincere, and other cultural groups rarely smile. Teachers should be aware that a smile does not always indicate a child's mood and thoughts in a given situation.

Figure 7.2 A Smile that Builds Relationships

Eye Contact

The act of looking someone in the eye generates much interest and discussion among students in many teacher education and human development classes. Western cultures see it as attentive, while in many Asian cultures eye contact is seen as disrespectful or a sign of deference. The term, the "Evil-eye" exists in some cultures, and people believe that staring at someone can hurt the person who is the focus of the eye contact.

Silence

It is interesting to experience silence and to observe people's levels of discomfort in a quiet room. Typically, the length of silence is related to comfort with silence. In some cultures, people learn that silence is awkward and should be quickly filled with commentary. In other cultures, speaking or responding too quickly after someone finished speaking can be interpreted as disrespectful behavior or lack of attention.

Hands-on Approach

Differences between early childhood classrooms and home cultures sometimes exist with regard to touching and using materials. On one level it is a question of independence vs. interdependence—should adults model how to use specific materials before children are invited to experience them, or are materials available for children so that they can do with them what they want? On another level, a classroom norm that materials in the classroom are to be shared and used by the group contributes to consideration of the wellbeing of the group and not simply an emphasis on individuals' wellbeing.

As you read the case study that follows, consider how Miki and the lead teacher, Mr. Lewis, reconciled expectations and assumptions about classroom values with cultural and linguistic realities that posed real challenges to what might be construed narrowly as school "success."

Case Study: Noel's Story

"There are 15 children in our Sheltered English Immersion classroom," Mr. Lewis told Miki, as they walked down the halls of the lower school. "All of them are native Haitian Creole speakers.

About half of the children and their families are new to the US, and the others have been here but have little to no *real* exposure to English. Oh, and they didn't go to preschool."

Miki's mouth felt dry and her palms felt wet, but she tried to keep a smile on her face. She could feel her heart beating fast in her chest. "Why am I so nervous?" she thought. "I don't even have the job yet. This is what I've been working and waiting for!" Miki tried to talk herself into a calmer state.

Mr. Lewis continued, "So the required MEPA testing—it's coming down from a really high level. The designated ELL teacher in the school didn't want to administer the test, but she had no choice. Our students here didn't do too well, so this year we're hoping to do better. Principal Wilson is coming down hard about preparing the kids for the MEPA and MELA-O. You say you've heard of these?"

Miki nodded her head and looked at the hallway walls, noticing all of the posters and flyers taped up. "The children walk past these everyday," Miki thought to herself, "and they have no idea what these words say, how to crack this code." She remembered learning about the Massachusetts proficiency and language exams that assess ELL students' reading, writing, and listening abilities. During her student teaching seminar, she and her classmates had many energetic conversations about the positive and negative aspects of bilingual education and standardized testing of ELL students.

Miki answered Mr. Lewis, "Yes, I'm familiar with them, but I've never administered them to students." Mr. Lewis nodded his head a few times, thinking. Then he said, "The questions are things that they assume every child is able to answer. Maybe some kinder-garteners don't know the answers, regardless of their English abilities! It's really a question of validity." Miki nodded her head a few times, thinking. "Yes . . . validity," she said, biting her lower lip. "What am I getting myself into?" she thought, nervously.

***

Her second week on the job felt a little more comfortable to Miki. She had been so thrilled to land a job in her town's public school, and since she was hired on such short notice, there hadn't been much time to feel nervous . . . or to feel prepared. As Mr. Lewis's teaching assistant, she could at least relax a bit, knowing that he got to call the shots.

She'd have to help Mr. Lewis administer the MELA-O though. Since it was an oral exam, she'd read it to the children and they'd have to respond. For the MEPA, the students would be able to take the tests themselves. Mr. Lewis told Miki that he didn't feel comfortable giving these tests to the kids—it felt unfair since many of them had such limited exposure to English.

So she and Mr. Lewis planned that for three weeks prior to the test, they'd have the kindergarteners practice test-taking skills, like filling in circles, or bubbles, like the ones they'd encounter on the exam. It still felt weird to Miki, to be testing kindergarteners—kindergarteners who couldn't read or speak much English. But the curriculum coordinator, Ms. Crow, had other expectations to deal with, like math packets and other curriculum mandates. "At least we'll be doing something proactive to help prepare the class before the exam. Maybe this kind of direct instruction will work!" Miki thought.

***

Most students in the Sheltered English Immersion kindergarten class couldn't read—they were functioning on a preK level. Many of them had relocated to Massachusetts after Hurricane Katrina destroyed their homes. So not only did the children need to cope with the trauma and confusion relating to the hurricane but they also had to figure out a strange new language in a strange new place. During the weeks before the MEPA, when a practice page was put in front of them, many of them looked very anxious. Mr. Lewis had handed control over these "practice sessions" to Miki. Mr. Lewis could speak Haitian Creole, and often did during class, but Miki couldn't speak a word of it. During these practice sessions students needed to use English to communicate with Miki, and most of the time the children looked at her with confused expressions as she read the instructions.

***

"They look so freaked out!" Miki told her roommate one evening, after a hard day at school. "They're confused that they can't look at each other's papers, too. All this time we've been trying to promote positive behaviors, and I mean, kindergarten is all about sharing." Miki's roommate, Jen, nodded sympathetically.

"One boy looked at the test and got really upset and anxious," Miki continued. "A large part of it is that he can't read yet, and he knows it, and he's used to having other kids help him. It created a lot of anxiety for him."

"Did you explain it to him?" Jen asked.

"No matter how many times the test was explained to him it didn't help. 'Do your best' didn't make a difference. I know he felt like he was going to get the wrong answer no matter what. It was frustrating for him and for us. I'm not sure what we could've done differently, other than simply not giving him the test." Miki felt tears welling in her eyes as she remembered Noel crying today. She felt as if the other children were making gains, but the gap between them and Noel was getting wider.

***

At the end of the year, coming from where he started to where he was now, Noel had made significant gains. Miki tried to be optimistic. "Maybe he's a 'late bloomer' or maybe he has a learning disability that will be identified," she thought. "He's definitely picked up speed."

Even authentic assessment practices and information obtained through direct assessment, such as classroom observations of children's behavior, can reflect mainstream biases. It is critical that school personnel make efforts to understand and respect the cultural backgrounds and home languages of all classroom members. In order to assess all children fairly and accurately, it is critical for school personnel to both reflect the culture and languages of the children they serve, as well as possess the requisite knowledge and skills to anticipate when specific adaptations are needed for children with diverse backgrounds (Espinosa, 2010).

Poverty

One area that cuts across cultural and linguistic boundaries, yet has substantial impact on children's learning and assessment, is poverty. "While there is no relationship between poverty and ability, the relationship between poverty and achievement is almost foolproof" (Riddile, 2010, p. 1). In response to American educational policies that focus attention on more efficient and visibly effective assessments, Heckman & Masterov (2007) criticize the trends in our society's policies and practices that traditionally look to the schools to fix the problems that originate in family environments. The authors argue that current policies such as NCLB perpetuate this trend, with dire consequences for disadvantaged families. "Schools can only work with what families give them," and the current emphasis on test scores in American schools ignores "the crucial noncognitive components of motivation, persistence and self-control that successful families foster in their children" (Heckman & Masterov, 2007, p. 34).

Heckman and Masterov present a unique argument in the assessment and accountability dialogue, by presenting an economic perspective. The authors suggest that investments will result in complementary gains. Investing in the lives of young children will impact school productivity, because teachers will encounter better prepared, higher-quality students. More productive and effective schools will therefore improve the quality of the American workforce. "Early skills breed later skills because early learning begets later learning. Both on theoretical and empirical grounds, at current levels of funding, investment in the young is warranted. Returns are highest for investments made at younger ages" (Heckman & Masterov, 2007, p. 24). Until the federal government addresses poverty on a national level, schools will continue to navigate through the policy waters and attempt to help all learners succeed through academic channels.

Differentiated Instruction or Universal Design

There are two entry-points into the "everyone can succeed" discussion. One begins with the premise that all children are different and teachers should use those differences as the anchor from which to design strategies and teach. The other begins with the premise that curricula can be designed so that everyone can learn, regardless of individual differences. While the endpoints are the same—success for all learners—the processes involved to bring about such success are somewhat different.

Differentiated Instruction

Teachers use data gained from assessments, and knowledge of students' learning preferences, language, and culture to provide students in the same class different teaching and learning strategies to address their specific needs. Because children learn best through different activities, differentiation involves a variety of strategies, such as small groups, team teaching, peer tutoring, learning centers, and specific accommodations. Teachers consider the most appropriate strategies to promote the greatest possible access to the instructional program (NCRTI, 2010).

Differentiated instruction works to eliminate the pressure children feel due to placement in groups based on abilities in specific subject areas. Even young children know which peers are "good at math" or are "really fast readers," and for years teachers have seen how tracking can result in self-fulfilling prophecies for some children. Depending on the group, high or low expectations can be implied by the activities involved, and it is often difficult for children to progress from group to group because of time constraints and assessment demands.

Figure 7.3 Engaging Children's Interests

Tiered Assignments

The idea behind tiered assignments is to provide students with parallel tasks that have different levels of depth, complexity, and abstractness, as well as different support elements or explicit guidance. All students work toward the same goal or outcome, and the differentiated tasks allow students to build on their prior knowledge and strengths while their work on the tasks provides them with appropriate challenges.

When preparing tiered assignments, teachers consider the material or content they want to teach, at the same time they consider how children will process the information and demonstrate their new knowledge. Typical levels that teachers use for their planning are: above grade level, on grade level, below grade level, and specific populations such as LEP. Table 7.3 presents an example of a tiered assignment that is distinguished by different levels. Methods of assessing differentiated assignments include specific rubrics for each level, checklists, self-evaluation, peer evaluation, and student-teacher mini-conferences.

Educators recognize that individual variation is the norm, not the exception (CAST, 2011). Young children are not born with an "average" identity, and therefore curricula must address the reality of learner variability. This includes learners with different abilities, backgrounds, and motivations to engage with classroom activities.

Table 7.3 Differentiated Instruction: Sample Tiered Assignment for Character Study

1. Above grade level

Choose a character from this book. It can be a character you like, or one that you don't like. Pretend you are eating lunch at a restaurant, and in walks the character! Describe what happens next.

2. On grade level

You are a news reporter about to interview your favorite character from the book. Ask the character:

- What his or her goals were in the story
- What the character would like people to know about him or her
- How he or she changed during the story
- One thing he or she said or did that was memorable in the story

3. Below grade level

Describe what character X looks like. Draw a picture of character X. What is the most important thing to know about character X? Draw a picture of character X doing something important in the story.

4. Limited English Proficient

Describe two characters in the story. Write down any words you can to describe the character. Tape record your answer with a friend.

Universal Design for Learning

The Center for Applied Special Technology (CAST) is a not-for-profit research and development organization, founded in 1984, with a mission to "expand learning opportunities for all individuals, especially those with disabilities, through the research and development of innovative, technology-based educational resources and strategies." The term Universal Design for Learning (UDL) was inspired by the universal design concept in architecture and product development, which aims to make physical environments and tools that are "usable" by as many people as possible (see http://www.cast.org/about/index.html).

As an organization CAST began trying to help individuals learn within the general education curriculum, despite disabilities. They later realized that the role of the environment was not considered in terms of how it identifies who is or isn't "disabled." The focus shifted onto curricula, and their limitations, specifically how those limitations "disable" learners (CAST, 2011). The researchers at CAST realized that the burden of students' success should be on the curricula, not the individual learners.

Universal design for learning is a framework for creating instructional goals, methods, materials, and assessments that work for all children. The goal is not to design a generic, one-size-fits-all solution, but approaches that are flexible to meet individual needs. The goal of education is to bring novice learners into the realm of experts, as learners who want to learn, who know how to apply strategies, and who are prepared for a lifetime of learning. The UDL framework helps educators meet this goal, by promoting understanding about how to create curricula that meet the needs of all learners.

Brain science supports the idea that individuals bring their own unique abilities, needs, and curiosity to classroom experiences. Every individual's set of skills reflects the functioning of brain networks. How children gather and organize information, express their ideas, and stay motivated and/or engaged during a task are some examples of functions UDL aims to optimize. Table 7.4 presents the three guiding principles of UDL, along with examples of each principle.

Teachers of young children help students develop skills all people need to thrive and succeed in a complex, diverse world. In the next chapter, we will look at how teachers can make sense of information gained through the assessment process and help children meet their goals.

Summary

In early childhood classrooms, children encounter materials and environments that can support their development and self-image, or exacerbate any uncertainty or anxiety they already have about their own competence. As children's cognitive development progresses, the cognitive conflicts that they experience relating to assumptions and biases can ultimately lead to new awareness about respect and difference. Anti-bias education

Table 7.4 Universal Design for Learning: Three Guiding Principles

---

1. *Provide multiple means of representation*
   Perception
   Language, expressions, and symbols
   Comprehension

2. *Provide multiple means of action and expression*
   Physical action
   Expression and communication
   Executive function

3. *Provide multiple means of engagement*
   Recruiting interest
   Sustaining effort and persistence
   Self-regulation

Adapted from: National Center on Universal Design for Learning (2010)
http://www.udlcenter.org

is both a philosophy and specific techniques for empowering children to challenge societal practices that support dominant biases in the United States. Teachers and children confront difficult issues in the classroom together, instead of avoiding them, to promote critical thinking and problem solving. In American classrooms, children who are poor, do not speak English well, or who are of a non-White ethnic background face obstacles in their education paths, much like children with physical and cognitive disabilities do. Strategies described as Differentiated Instruction have been highly regarded as a way of promoting learning for all learners. This is a fundamental goal of Universal Design for Learning.

Now What?

1. You're organizing books on the kindergarten classroom bookshelves and notice a lot of princess books—*Cinderella*, *Snow White*, and *The princess and the pea*, to name a few. How could you frame a group discussion with the children about the themes in those stories? What are some big concepts you might expect to emerge, and what are some that the children might need some guidance to understand?
2. You are a principal of a suburban elementary school. This year your school did not make Annual Yearly Progress, as required by NCLB. How do you make it clear to families that children's learning and thinking are progressing in ways that might not be visible in terms of standardized test scores, but are vastly important in terms of students' self-images and actions as members of the community?
3. Think back to your own early childhood years in school. How were holidays and family traditions celebrated? What do you think is the most sensitive, appropriate way for schools to recognize family traditions and national customs?

Avenues for Inquiry

Educational Equity Center

The website for the Educational Equity Center promotes bias-free learning in schools and outside of classrooms. The organization strives to "eliminate inequities based on gender, race/ethnicity, disability, and level of family income" through professional development opportunities and community outreach.

http://www.edequity.org

IDEA

This website provides a vast amount of resources related to *IDEA* 2004 legislation, intervention and evaluation, identification of specific learning disabilities, and connections to other laws and regulations. Featuring video clips and links, this interactive site is designed to engage and inform visitors.

http://www.idea.ed.gov

Teaching for Change

The Teaching for Change website features resources for families and professionals dedicated to transforming schools into "centers of justice." The site provides links to professional development, as well as publications and parent organizing opportunities.

http://www.teachingforchange.org

8

Putting It All Together

Not everything that can be counted counts, and not everything that counts can be counted.

(Albert Einstein, physicist)

There's a lot of people using hammers when they should be using screwdrivers.
(Stephen Gould, retired principal and professor, 2011)

A colleague whom I admire was recently speaking with me about his years as an elementary school principal. He said that the most important piece of the assessment process is "putting it all together" (S. Gould, personal communication, August 16, 2011). Specifically, he spoke about a teacher's disposition to want to know more and solve problems, "as opposed to the attitude that you're 'supposed' to 'do' assessment or that every person is an individual. It takes a whole set of keys to figure out how to unlock something." That attitude about assessment is, of course, most empowered when supported by a principal and school district with a similar stance toward assessment—unlocking information about children that will enable all stakeholders to work in the interest of children's successes in school and life.

Teachers do have a good amount of autonomy with regard to how they communicate information to families and specialists (McAfee, Leong, & Bodrova, 2004). This chapter explores several aspects of making sense of data and the new understandings that result from noticing. Opening channels with children, families, and others—forming meaningful relationships—helps educators put assessment puzzle pieces together, in their efforts to help children reach their goals, both academic and social. Practitioners increase the quality of their interactions with children and families by creating a positive, responsive climate that values multiple perspectives. Engaging in rich, bi-directional feedback on a consistent basis with children, parents, specialists, and administrators strengthens communication about assessment matters and simultaneously promotes social, academic, language, and technology skills. The collaborative process helps children feel more engaged with educators and with each other, and therefore children feel more comfortable tackling new challenges, trusting that people will be there to support them (Jacobs & Crowley, 2010).

Evaluating Data

Teachers evaluate data every day, in all of its various forms—formal and informal assessment data, formative and summative data. For formal assessments, such as standardized tests, reports are typically generated and sent to the district offices for dissemination, which may or may not reach families' mailboxes. In terms of informal assessments, teachers have many opportunities to evaluate and convey information gained through formative assessments, such as the use of letters or email communication to families, phone calls, documentation panels, and other electronic/digital means to be discussed later in this chapter.

Because of regulations aligned with schools' accountability efforts, "much information is combined with reports from other schools and centers and becomes public information, available to everyone. Sometimes it's posted on the Internet, sometimes it is headlined in newspapers and on television" (McAfee, Leong, & Bodrova, 2004, p.74). It is therefore critical that practitioners protect their notes, test documents, and drafts of reports in the classroom before and after ongoing assessment practices are carried out in the classroom.

Confidentiality and Care

One of the most important measures for practitioners to take and maintain is attention to confidentiality. Teachers must always consider confidential assessment materials private, and treat them in such a way that only authorized individuals (school officials, parents, the child) are allowed access to them. Public documentation of individual and group work is a vastly different category, in which the public nature is intended to inspire and extend learning and understanding. The public documentation is intended to be public. Private assessment data is not assumed to be for public consumption unless confidentiality precautions are taken. Any information about children's families, medical information, test scores, anecdotal records, and progress reports should be kept in a locked file cabinet or other secure place.

Teachers must also be mindful of the language they use in writing up evaluative statements or reports. For example, when a teacher is describing a child's behavior, the description should be rich with specific, vivid details, rather than with generalizations that can be misinterpreted and misconstrued. A report that describes a child as "very inattentive and hard to control" is not particularly useful for planning successful interventions or adjusting the curriculum. A teacher who presents running records that describe a child's frequent wiggling, touching classmates' hair and bodies, and the number of times a teacher needs to redirect or sit one-on-one with the child is much more specific. Teachers must also remember to refrain from interpreting or diagnosing behavior during a naturalistic observation or running record. Hypotheses and judgments come about as a result of the written material, but should not be recorded within the evaluation.

Evaluating pencil and paper data is quite different than evaluating video clips or children's drawings. A collaborative process of the sort described in Chapter 5, Looking at Students' Work, helps reduce the chance of assumptions and biases influencing interpretation. The co-founders of Videatives (www.videatives.com), George Forman and Ellen Hall, have painstakingly and methodically analyzed and archived hundreds of video clips of young children. Their analyses of children's behavior are presented alongside video clips, and therefore illustrate the competence of young children, as well as things they do not yet know or are unable to do. The collaborative approach, using video clips as an alternative to standardized assessments, offers opportunities for teachers to view and review an exchange between children or focus on a child's actions, while sitting next to a colleague and discussing thoughts and hypotheses that spring from evidence in the videos. Such hypotheses are important to consider during the writing of reports and IEPs. While not necessarily included in formal reports, hypotheses that grow out of assessment measures lead to continued, shared investigations and understandings.

Writing Reports and IEPs

For some reason putting something in writing scares people, or at the very least makes them nervous. There is, at times, a veiled threat attached to someone saying, "Can I get that in writing?" Putting thoughts in writing is a serious business, because as mentioned earlier, teachers' writing can be used in public ways, ranging from letters to magazine articles to formal reports. When parents receive a report from their child's teacher, they tend to worry, "Is there a problem?" "Is my child normal?" Parents and caregivers have a lot to make sense of as they evaluate data about their children, and written reports provided by practitioners are helpful to bridge the assessment and suggested intervention or action. While there are a number of different styles of reporting information to parents, the most common forms of reports are progress reports, also known as report cards, that go out to families several times a year from a child's primary teacher.

Progress Reports

Consider the three elementary school progress reports presented in Figures 8.1, 8.2, and 8.3. They are actual progress reports from three members of a family, and represent three generations of learners. The progress report presented in Figure 8.1 was written in the academic year 1955–56. The progress report presented in Figure 8.2 was written in the academic year 1984–85, and the one presented in Figure 8.3 was written in the academic year 2007–08. It is interesting to look at each of the progress reports and to consider several elements of each one, in terms of the explicit and implicit messages being communicated to parents.

The back cover of the first progress report, Figure 8.1a, features a letter from the Great Neck, NY Superintendent of Schools, explaining to parents in a personal manner the purpose and tone of the progress report. It includes language such as "growth and development," "grow at his own best rate and in his own pattern," and "friendliness and cooperation among parents and teachers." Neither of the subsequent progress reports features a personalized message from a district level official. What is a potential benefit of having such a personal message included with the progress report?

A comparison of the different presentations of subject matter and content area sections in the three progress reports yields some fascinating information and raises important questions. First, in Figures 8.1b and 8.1c, the different categories are delineated for each area. The choices that a teacher may check are "satisfactory progress" or "little progress," but progress nonetheless, based on a teacher's assessment of a child's potential. It is assumed that children will grow and change over the year. Note the number of categories under "Reading" (5) and "Mathematics" (3). Note the fine print in Figure 8.1c, which states that the items listed under "work habits" have been discussed through "cooperative evaluation" between teacher and pupil. What is one possible intention behind making explicit the relationship that underlies that cooperative effort?

Dear Parents:

This report represents an attempt to appraise the growth and development of your child, both in school subjects and in desirable social traits and attitudes.

Careful teaching will help the child to grow at his own best rate and in his own pattern. Parents and teachers can help most when they help the child to *want* to grow.

This report serves as an inventory of *this child's* progress, not as a method of measuring one child's growth against another's.

It is known from experience that a spirit of friendliness and co-operation among parents and teachers helps to provide a better learning and growing environment for children. Parent and teacher conferences provide opportunities for developing a more complete and mutual understanding of children than is possible through written notes, telephone calls or "report cards."

Twice during each school year, several afternoons are set aside so that teachers may invite parents to visit the school for such conferences.

Requests from parents for additional conferences are welcomed. It is always best to arrange for additional conferences or for a classroom visitation well in advance, through a written note to the teacher.

Superintendent of Schools

Figure 8.1a Report Card 1955–56

	WINTER		SPRING	
THIS REPORT IS BASED UPON OUR EVALUATION OF *Joan's* INDIVIDUAL ABILITIES	SATISFACTORY PROGRESS	LITTLE PROGRESS	SATISFACTORY PROGRESS	LITTLE PROGRESS

READING

Shows growth in:

reading with understanding	✓		✓	
developing reading interests	✓		✓	
reading for the enjoyment of others		✓	✓	
acquiring basic skills	✓		✓	
using books as sources of information	✓		✓	

OTHER LANGUAGE SKILLS

Shows growth in:

speaking purposefully		✓	✓	
expressing written thoughts	✓		✓	
writing legibly and easily	✓		✓	
developing accurate spelling in all written work	✓		✓	
contributing to group discussions	✓		✓	

SOCIAL STUDIES AND SCIENCE

Shows growth in:

understanding of the development of community life	✓		✓	
understanding of the physical world	✓		✓	

MATHEMATICS

Shows growth in:

acquiring basic skills	✓		✓	
use of numbers in meaningful situations	✓		✓	
understanding of the meaning of numbers	✓		✓	

Figure 8.1b Report Card 1955–56

	WINTER		SPRING	
During this reporting period the items listed under work habits and social attitudes have been used as the basis of evaluation by the teacher and pupil. The check represents the teacher's judgment based upon that cooperative evaluation.	SATISFACTORY PROGRESS	LITTLE PROGRESS	SATISFACTORY PROGRESS	LITTLE PROGRESS

SOCIAL ATTITUDES

Shows growth in:

carrying out responsibilities	✓		✓	
considering others	✓		✓	
accepting group decisions	✓		✓	
listening attentively	✓		✓	
cooperating in group activities	✓		✓	
caring for school and personal property	✓		✓	
relating out of school experiences to classroom activities	✓		✓	
making independent and wise decisions	✓		✓	

PHYSICAL EDUCATION

Shows growth in:

physical-mental co-ordination	✓		✓	
developing basic skills (running, jumping, catching, throwing)	✓		✓	
participating in group games	✓		✓	
participating in rhythmic activities (creative, folk dance)	✓		✓	

WORK — STUDY HABITS

Shows growth in:

following directions	✓		✓	
working independently	✓		✓	
planning and completing work	✓		✓	

Figure 8.1c Report Card 1955–56

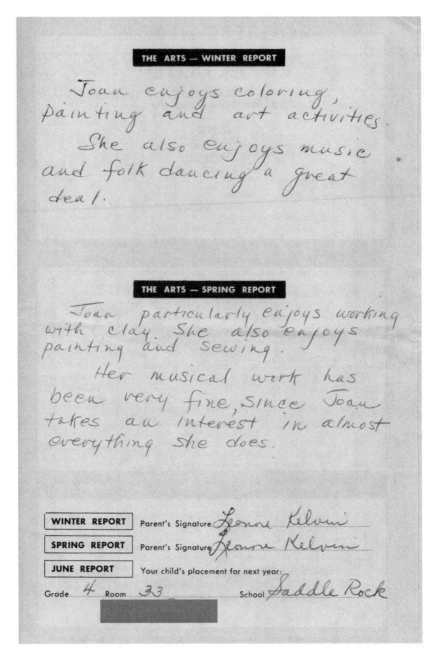

Figure 8.1d Report Card 1955–56

PROGRESS REPORT

KINDERGARTEN

2ND

REPORTING
PERIOD

This Progress Report on your Kindergarten child is designed to provide a profile on demonstrated skill areas: social/emotional development, physical development, social science/science, art/music, reading/language development, and math development. A three point scale is used to summarize how frequently your child has demonstrated a specific skill during the reporting period:

Scale Values	Interpretation
E	*Most of the time, your child has demonstrated the skill*
S	*Some of the time, your child has demonstrated the skill*
N	*So far, your child has not demonstrated the skill*
-- (dash)	*Your child is not being marked in this area at this time*

Your child's Scale Value (E, S, N, or --) represents consistency in skill performance which is not necessarily attributable to ability or interest, or lack thereof. For further interpretation, if required, you are invited to contact your child's teacher.

KINDERGARTEN PROGRESS REPORT

Student __Alex   Davidson__   Teacher _____

School __Montematoga__

Date __April, 1985__

An "X" in the appropriate space marks the
Scale Value of your child's performance.

	KEY to Scale Values
E	*Most of the time, your child has demonstrated the skill*
S	*Some of the time, your child has demonstrated the skill*
N	*So far, your child has not demonstrated the skill*
--	*Your child is not being marked in this area at this time*

SCALE VALUES

E	S	N	--
X			
X			
X			
X			
X			
X			
X			
X			
X			
X			

SOCIAL / EMOTIONAL DEVELOPMENT
Is cooperative with others
Has positive involvement in group activities
Respects the rights, property, and ideas of others
Shows self-control
Accepts responsibility
Meets new tasks with confidence
Accepts the consequences of own behavior
Listens for and follows directions
Has attention span adequate to complete tasks
Works independently
Uses learning materials properly

E	S	N	--
X			
X			

PHYSICAL DEVELOPMENT
Uses small muscles with control and coordination
Uses large muscles with control and coordination

E	S	N	--
X			
X			

SOCIAL SCIENCE / SCIENCE
Participates in social science activities
Shows interest in science found in everyday life

E	S	N	--
X			
X			

ART / MUSIC
Enjoys experimenting with art media
Participates in music activities

E	S	N	--
X			
X			
X			
X			
X			
X			
X			
X			
X			
X			

READING / LANGUAGE DEVELOPMENT
Communicates ideas and experiences to others
Uses complete sentences to express thoughts
Can recall parts of a story in sequence
Can recall personal information (address, telephone no., etc.)
Can tell a story from pictures
Recognizes lower-case letters
Knows initial consonant sounds
Can distinguish rhyming words
Visually discriminates likenesses and differences
Uses a left-to-right progression

E	S	N	--
X			
X			
X			
X			

MATH DEVELOPMENT
Makes simple comparisons, using size, weight, length, and height
Knows basic shapes: circle, square, triangle, rectangle
Recognizes number symbols
Uses numbers with understanding

2d Reporting Period
KDGN Checklist 2
F-1726 C2

Tran Davidson
Signature of Parent

PARENT COPY

	READING SKILLS	MATHEMATICS SKILLS
ACHIEVES ABOVE THE AVERAGE OF WHAT IS EXPECTED OF STUDENTS IN KINDERGARTEN	X	X
ACHIEVES AT THE AVERAGE OF WHAT IS EXPECTED OF STUDENTS IN KINDERGARTEN		
ACHIEVES BELOW THE AVERAGE OF WHAT IS EXPECTED OF STUDENTS IN KINDERGARTEN		

Figure 8.2a–b Report Card 1984–85

Belmont Public Schools
Kindergarten Pupil Evaluation

This progress report is a communication tool which fosters the home/school partnership, so essential for academic, social, and personal growth. It reflects the student's development at this specific period in a continuum of lifelong learning.

Pupil's Name: Matthew ▇▇▇▇▇▇▇▇   School: Wellington _____

Teacher: Amy ▇▇▇▇▇▇   School year: 2007-2008 _____

                   Parent's Signature: _____

Key: N – Needs time to develop   2 – winter assessment (term 2)
         A – Acquiring skill with support   3 – spring assessment (term 3)
         D – Developing independence
         I – Independently/consistent

Personal and Social Growth
N   A   D   I

                                   Comments:

<----------------------------2,3--> Shows positive attitude toward self
<----------------------------2,3--> Shows positive attitude toward school and learning-----(seems to enjoy school)
<----------------------------2,3--> Follows school rules and limits
<----------------------------2,3--> Displays physical self-control
<----------------------------2,3--> Displays emotional self-control-----(can become upset with changes to routine)
<----------------------------2,3--> Handles transitions well and follows school routines
<----------------------------2,3--> Interacts appropriately with others
<--------------------------2-3---> Takes acceptable risks-----(needs some reassurance at times)
<----------------------------2,3--> Respects individual differences
<----------------------------2,3--> Accepts responsibility for behavior
<--------------------------2-3---> Is able to organize self

Learning Skills and Attitudes
N   A   D   I

<----------------------------2,3--> Accepts responsibility for learning
<----------------------------2,3--> Demonstrates effort
<----------------------------2,3--> Values own work-----(Matthew shows pride in his work)
<----------------------------2,3--> Works cooperatively
<----------------------------2,3--> Works independently
<----------------------------2,3--> Uses materials with care and cleans up after self
<--------------------------2-3---> Ask help of an adult when appropriate-----(can hesitate at times)
<----------------------------2,3--> Makes good use of learning activities
<----------------------------2,3--> Questions, investigates, shows curiosity
<--------------------------2-3---> Remains focused on task-----(needs some support getting/staying on task at times)
<----------------------------2,3--> Shows partiality to left/right
<----------------------------2,3--> Shows control in use of crayon, pencil, paint brush, scissors

3/2008

Matthew continues to work well within our learning community. Although Matthew can be shy at times, he is friendly, considerate, and compassionate. He demonstrates a consistent, strong effort. Matthew seems to enjoy school and is a happy boy. He knows 23 of the first 25 sight words, has gained a strong foundation in phonemic awareness, and is an early reader reading beyond a Kindergarten level. Matthew is very strong in math and enjoys working with numbers. I am looking forward to Matthew's continued growth in Kindergarten this year.

Kindergarten Pupil Evaluation   Page 2

Pupil's Name: _____

Key: N – Needs time to develop   2 – winter assessment (term 2)
         A – Acquiring skill with support   3 – spring assessment (term 3)
         D – Developing independence
         I – Independently/consistent

Literacy

N   A   D   I

                                                                              Comments:

<----------------------------2,3--> Demonstrates clear language pattern
<----------------------------2,3--> Uses appropriate vocabulary
<----------------------------2,3--> Reflects upon and engages in class discussion
<------------------------2--3--------> Retells details and sequence of stories
<----------------------------2--3--> Attends during group meeting-----(can lose focus or become distracted by others)
<----------------------------2--3--> Follows multi-step directions
<----------------------------2,3--> Recognizes first and last name in print
<----------------------------2,3--> Writes first and last name
<----------------------------2,3--> Names uppercase letters
<----------------------------2,3--> Names lowercase letters
<----------------------------2,3--> Works from left to right
<----------------------------2,3--> Writes letters from memory
<----------------------------2--3--> Selects a topic for writing-----(needs some support at times)
<----------------------------2,3--> Conveys story ideas through illustrations
<----------------------------2,3--> Conveys story ideas through phonetic spelling
<----------------------------2,3--> Recognizes conventions of print in text
<----------------------------2-3--> Organizes own story in logical sequence (beginning, middle, end)-----(story can lose focus)
<----------------------------2--3--> Interprets own writing and shares with others
<----------------------------2,3--> Aware that print carries meaning
<----------------------------2--3--> Uses strategies for beginning reading-----(some ind., more w/ support, attend more carefully)

Mathematics

N   A   D   I

<----------------------------2,3--> Sorts objects by size, shape and/or color
<----------------------------2,3--> Understands patterns: matches, extends, creates
<----------------------------2,3--> Recognizes numbers 0-20-----(30/30 and beyond)
<----------------------------2,3--> Counts 0-100-----(and beyond)
<----------------------------2--3--> Counts by 5's and 10's to 100
<----------------------------2,3--> Demonstrates one to one correspondence
<----------------------------2,3--> Associates numbers 0-20 with corresponding groups of objects
<----------------------------2,3--> Uses numbers to record data
<----------------------------2,3--> Represents addition and subtraction with objects
<----------------------------2,3--> Understands number stories-----(records w/ minimal support for math signs)
<----------------------------2,3--> Interprets tables, charts and graphs
<----------------------------3---> Uses standard and non-standard devices to measure

                                                          Assigned to grade: ___1__

6/2008

Matthew has had a very successful year in Kindergarten. He has grown both socially and academically. Matthew is reading above grade level and is aware of and able to apply many literacy skills and strategies. He is gaining confidence as a reader. Matthew knows all 25 sight words and is proficient in letter naming fluency, phonemic segmentation fluency, and nonsense word fluency. Matthew is become strong in math operations and number sense. Matthew is an eager learner. I enjoyed working with Matthew very much and I wish him continued success in first grade.

Figure 8.3a–b Report Card 2007–08

How does that relate to responsibility? Figure 8.1d shows the open response section for the arts. Someone involved in the design of this progress report form considered it important that the arts were assessed using qualitative feedback, rather than quantitative all-or-nothing check marks. How is this significant? (It is perhaps interesting to note that the child about whom this progress report was written later became an artist and art teacher.)

The second progress report features a brief explanation about the rating scale, which is linked to demonstration of skills, evidenced "most of the time," "some of the time," or "not demonstrated" (see Figure 8.2a). Although the initials E, S, and N are used, there is no key that explains the word that those letters represent. However, the words "excellent," "satisfactory," and "not satisfactory" come to mind. Consider the sentence, "Your child's Scale Value (E, S, N, or –) represents consistency in skill performance which is not necessarily attributable to ability or interest, or lack thereof." What is performance linked to, if not ability or interest? The categories under Reading/Language Development (10) and Math Development (4) reflect an increase in attention paid to those two content areas. Finally, note the small box in the corner that introduces the element of competition, whether a child is at, above, or below average in reading and math skills. Why the specific focus on those two areas?

The third progress report features a very different format—a continuum for each area, moving from "Needs time to develop" to "Acquiring skill with support" to "Developing independence" to "Independently/consistent." This, according to the brief comments at the top of Figure 8.3a reflects a child's development over the year, which is but one year in a continuum of "lifetime learning." Note the number of Literacy categories (20) and Mathematics categories (12). How have the categories, so much more general in 1956, become so much more specific today? Is this helpful to parents and caregivers, or is less sometimes more valuable and meaningful?

Routine progress reports provide insights into what is valued by educators, schools, and the broader education community. As teachers communicate with families throughout the year, opportunities to show examples of children's progress through the use of documentation serves to complement the ongoing work and communicates progress for individuals and the larger group. This helps reduce unpleasant surprises if problems are suspected, but also celebrates the power of ordinary learning moments that are quite extraordinary for children.

Over time, if a teacher's routine observations and assessments indicate need for closer investigation into something specific, progress reports serve as one source of documentation that can support the need for testing or other evaluation services. As discussed in Chapter 7, Individual Education Programs (IEPs) are developed to support the specific needs of individual students, whether those needs are emotional, physical, or academic. An IEP is a written document, similar to a contract, which details an educational plan for a child to succeed under the supervision and guidance from the family, teachers and professionals, and administrators. These plans are considered to be binding documents between schools and families, in the interest of students' success. As you read the case study below, consider how an opportunity for partnership and communication between educators and parents might be strengthened in situations where a potential problem warrants specific attention and intervention.

Case Study: Everything's Fine (Motor)

Christina was nervous about the IEP meeting on that late May morning. As if having twins wasn't enough trouble, now she had to deal with *this*! "Well," she thought, "at least it's not for both of them!"

Christina's neighbor Elizabeth, an IEP advocate, volunteered to come to Caleb's meeting. Because Elizabeth went to IEP meetings several times a week as part of her job, Christina was grateful to have a seasoned expert in her corner. Christina had given Elizabeth the whole history—Caleb had been having a hard time in preschool for months, and no matter what strategies she or his teacher Jessica tried, he still had a hard time staying focused, sitting still, and keeping his hands to himself. His twin brother Hayden, while also "a handful," didn't seem to have the same impulse control issues. The other day Jessica had come over to Christina, sheepishly, and told Christina that Caleb had "taken down" a girl at recess. While Christina was indeed nervous about what the IEP team meeting might reveal about Caleb, she was also really relieved that people were finally taking her concerns seriously and that help was on the way.

***

The IEP meeting felt surreal to Christina—a blur at some times and almost slow motion at other times. Seated around the table were Christina and Elizabeth, Caleb's teacher Jessica, the school director, the occupational therapist, the physical therapist, and the town's special education director. She found it hard to focus on what everyone was saying. The town specialists had done an Occupational Therapy (OT) and Physical Therapy (PT) evaluation, but that was all they had covered. They hadn't done any behavioral or other screening. While Elizabeth had suggested getting Caleb a private evaluation, Christina couldn't bear to think of the expense associated with that, so she decided to see what the team proposed. Now that she was listening to the experts' opinions, she was beginning to regret not having Caleb evaluated someplace else.

Although the OT and PT specialists validated Christina's and Jessica's concerns and observations, they focused mainly on Caleb's fine motor skills, specifically his lack of skill cutting with scissors. They recommended that Caleb receive 45 minutes of physical therapy one day a week, beginning in September. "That's it?!" Christina thought. She wasn't sure if she'd blurted it out loud or merely thought it in her head. Judging by the impassive expressions of the people at the table, she realized she hadn't outwardly expressed her disbelief. The therapists said that, if Caleb hadn't displayed the fine motor "stuff," they wouldn't have recommended services at all, because his academic abilities were fine. The preschool director commented reassuringly, "He's such an intelligent boy!" Christina thought, "As if that's supposed to make this all ok?" and tried not to cry. Elizabeth suggested that they take a short break, and when the others left the room, she advised Christina not to sign the IEP form.

**

"Here's a kid who has issues, and because he's intelligent they're not willing to do anything!" Christina was furious. Elizabeth was driving them home. "That's not even my concern at all! If you ask me, I don't care if he never uses scissors until he's 18! Four-and-a-half-year-olds and scissors—not a great idea!" Elizabeth calmly replied, "That's not your main concern at all—you're concerned about Caleb's behavior, and controlling his impulses. I understand, and we'll try to help them understand, too."

"Right! What are we supposed to do—wait until something happens and it *does* disrupt the classroom, interfere with his academics, or making friends? This doesn't make sense. How long do we wait?" Christina asked.

Elizabeth answered, "That seems to be their narrow focus—fine motor skills—instead of the bigger picture. You have time to think things over and plan before the next meeting. We'll think of some options to offer at the table."

**

At the second IEP team meeting, Christina felt a bit more prepared. She and Elizabeth had talked about a plan of action. They decided that Christina should ask for more than one day a week of services for Caleb. She was also eager to start as soon as possible, because it was already almost the end of the school year. She was worried that if they waited too long, or asked for too much, they'd lose their chance.

The occupational therapist, Erika, didn't think it would be possible to have Caleb come for more than one day a week, stating, "We planned for the 45-minute session because we know it's going to take him some time to settle down before we can actually do anything with him. Sessions are usually 30 minutes, but if we spent 15 minutes waiting for Caleb to settle down, then half the session time would be lost."

"So you agree that he has a hard time keeping still and focused? Then why aren't you addressing it?" asked Christina.

"Yes, we've noticed that, as we mentioned last time," Erika said. "We share your concerns. But we're not sure about something like ADHD or sensory processing at this time. We'll begin services in September and review again as a team in November. We can reassess things at that time."

***

Later that day, Christina filled her mother in about details of the second IEP meeting. Christina summed up a few of the main headlines. "They mentioned ADHD, and hinted that he might have some sensory processing issues, but they won't do any further testing until November at the earliest."

"To be honest," her mother said, "I'm embarrassed because I've never noticed the fine motor issue, and I'm with the boys all the time."

"Me either!" said Christina. "And I'm with them more than you are! It's so frustrating for the teachers, for me, for you, and everyone who's with him all the time and sees this stuff."

"Well at least they agreed to begin this summer, instead of waiting until September," shrugged Christina's mom. "That's one good thing."

"Yup," sighed Christina. "It just doesn't make sense."

Utilizing Technology

The process of writing reports for many children has been made simpler and quicker through the use of technology. Software has been designed to help facilitate evaluations, and professional development training is available year-round and at various conferences for educators who wish to learn about the latest assessment product or strategy. Researchers have identified three purposes of the use of technology in assessment:

1. to collect information with greater reliability and validity;
2. to collect it more efficiently;
3. to provide a mechanism to feed into instructional efforts resulting from the assessment.

A challenge for educators is "being able to keep abreast of all of the innovations that can help [teachers] perform assessments" (Shermis & DiVesta, 2011, p. 237). This challenge is complicated by the temptation educators face, in not attempting to use technology for the sake of the pretty colors on the screen or because a new computer seems like a fun tool/toy.

Researchers acknowledge that a primary role of technology in assessment should revolve around a child realizing her potential across specific developmental areas. Particularly for young children, but true for all children, assessment must involve more than standardized tests. Technology provides tools to create and refine documentation that supports a specific argument about something significant that individuals or groups of children have learned. In the current culture that demands evidence of children's progress and learning, technology is a critical tool for making sense of assessment data.

When educators hear the word "technology," many images spring to mind: CD-ROMs or DVDs and other disks, video cameras, audio recorders, PowerPoint presentations or the more old-fashioned yet tried and true acetate "slides." Teachers can work with one child, a small group of children, or the whole class in the use of technology. Children are able to incorporate more than a two-dimensional assessment tool into their overall learning profile, by combining visual representations as well as hard copies of actual classroom work. Technology provides opportunities to preserve and examine a child's growth over time, which affords an opportunity for teachers to emphasize process over product, and delay of gratification.

Technology and assessment experts gently caution that technology is sometimes used for the sake of having a new tool or gizmo in the classroom. Such educators don't necessarily consider the best methods for answering specific questions about children's abilities and potential. They also might not consider the most accurate and efficient ways to track students' growth over time. Educator Grant Wiggins says of portfolio assessment, "Well, that's fine for the student, but there's hardly another human being other than the kid's family that wants to wade through all that." He continues, offering that technology serves a critical role when used to store data, manage data and evaluation reports, and store materials and files. Technology archives offer possible ways for students to connect face-to-face as well as in virtual environments (Grant Wiggins; http://www.edutopia.org/grant-wiggins-assessment#graph2).

As the most important, primary environment for children is their home environment, classroom teachers of young children should take advantage of all opportunities to engage families and the wider community in communication (see Table 8.1).

Table 8.1 Ten Tips for Involving Families through Internet-Based Communication

1. Create a classroom website.
Include items such as calendar, family handbook, announcements, permission slips, wish lists, and volunteer opportunities on a password-protected site. (See http://sites.google.com, www.webs.com, and www.wikispaces.com)

2. Send individual emails to share positive information about a particular child's activities and accomplishments.
Teachers and parents often communicate about challenging issues, and it is important to establish a relationship that includes positive, spontaneous communication.

3. Post photo stories on the class website.
Photos help families understand the processes through which children learn.

4. Provide at-home educational activities.
The classroom website can help families access technology to extend classroom learning.

5. Create a family response link or forum on the webpage to elicit comments, questions, and feedback.
Parents can comment on their child's progress using a brief online form or survey.

6. Establish and moderate a family support discussion forum.
Teachers can moderate a discussion about a topic of interest, such as assessment.

7. Communicate logistic information through group emails.
Group emails provide an alternative to other informal communication.

8. Ensure families' access to technology.
Apply for funding from public and private organizations that provide laptops or other preK-12 grants. (See http://computersforlearning.gov and www.teachersnetwork.org/Grants/grants_technology.htm)

9. Provide opportunities for families to increase their technology skills.
Provide brief orientation to and demonstrations with class website during Open House and parent-teacher conferences.

10. Set aside time for technology-based communication.
Teachers can seek out opportunities for professional development and training to learn new technology tools. Families may be invited to share their technology expertise with others.

Adapted from: Mitchell, Foulger, & Wetzel (2009:46–49).

Communicating with Families, Administrators, and Legislators

Many parents of young children, while interested in their children's progress, worry about their responsibilities and how those align with a teacher's proposed goals for children and rules supported and emphasized in the schools as a whole. One way that teachers and parents can build a valuable partnership with others is to keep to a systematic approach to technology use in the classroom. Working with families as a major source of information that is useful for assessment means that teachers must encourage and scaffold technology use through online discussions, notes or personal records, and other technology tools.

Most schools and child care centers have their own historical means of sharing child assessment information. Family conferences, written progress reports, and portfolios of children's work are typical for preK and older "young" children. Formal progress reports, including report cards, are usually adjusted in the primary grades to provide a thread of consistency. Many teachers involve children in discussions about technology and its uses in the classroom activities (McAfee, Leong, & Bodrova, 2004, p.75), which warrants special attention.

Ethical Considerations

The National Association for the Education of Young Children (NAEYC) has developed specific statements focusing on ethical responsibilities that the organization deems important. The Code of Ethical Conduct Section II—Ethical Responsibilities to Families—features two specific points that encourage teachers to reach out to families to nurture relationships between all groups in the classroom. The points are typed as follows:

> Develop relationships of mutual trust and create partnerships with families served.
>
> (I-2.2)

> Welcome all family members and encourage them to participate in the program.
>
> (I-2.3)

One of the simplest and most routine ways to involve families in children's assessments and nurture trust is to participate in parent–teacher conferences that occur several times during the school year.

Family Conference

It is most common to share assessment results and evaluations with families during parent–teacher conferences, in which formal progress reports or report cards are discussed. Teachers can lay the groundwork for two-way communication with families before the school year begins, by sending out parent questionnaires or online surveys to gather some preliminary information. Figure 8.4 provides an example of a parent questionnaire that can be sent out in the weeks before school begins. Prior to a scheduled parent–teacher conference, teachers can send out brief forms asking parents about their goals for the conference and any questions or concerns that they would like to discuss. Cultural and linguistic differences between families and teachers may affect routine

---

Student's name: _____

Parents' name(s):   _____

1. What are your child's strengths?

2. What do you think your child needs to work on?

3. What goals do you have (social and/or academic) for your child in 1st grade?

4. What are some of your child's interests?

5. Does your child participate in any after-school activities? Which ones?

6. If you need to redirect your child, what seems to work best?

7. Does your child have any allergies?

8. Preferred phone number or email address _____

9. What concerns or questions do you have about 1st grade?

Thank you! Feel free to attach an additional sheet of paper with any additional comments.

Figure 8.4 Parent Questionnaire

communication, so preparation using written materials as well as verbal communication is helpful.

In general it is better for educators to focus on one or two educational or developmental issues during a family conference. Further, a letter to families, written in clear and simple language, may present any specific assessment terms with which family members may not be familiar. It is important to remember that while family members and teachers may be highly skilled in specific content areas, that does not assume that they know and understand terms such as those discussed in Chapter 4, or child assessment processes (McAfee, Leong, & Bodrova, 2004).

Empowering Parents and Caregivers

It is helpful for parents to be able to place their children's progress and performance in context through the presentation of evidence that has been collected about a specific child or group of children. Such evidence may serve as the foundation for continued discussions with parents. Specific evidence, organized and ready to use as examples of a child's strengths or areas that need some extra time or support, empowers families to choose a course of action that will support their child's growth. Parents can look through a child's portfolio, and see which pages are "marked" for parents' attention. Anecdotal records, checklists of specific skills, and examples of ways that a child has helped other children are much more meaningful than a written comment along the lines of, "Steve is really good at baseball" (McAfee, Leong, & Bodrova, 2004).

Educators should also be aware of the pressures parents experience and place on themselves out of a sense of duty to implement whatever strategies are determined priorities for young children. If parents are asked to provide their child with some assistance or extra support in the home, they should receive specific, reasonable suggestions for what they can do. For instance, if a child is making excellent progress with reading and could benefit from some extra support at home, simply suggesting that a child needs "some help" is less motivating and empowering than showing families the results of specific assessments to best inform family members of what they can do to support their child (ibid.). "The wealth of information [teachers] have about each child will enable [them] to talk with families knowledgably and confidently, as well as to seek their perspectives. They will appreciate that [teachers] really know their child" (ibid.).

Specialists/Administrators

Having assessment information well organized and ready to share with others best prepares and empowers teachers to work with specialists and administrators. When teachers are able to provide specialists and administrators with specific and relevant examples from classroom assessment efforts, they have a better platform for showing the merits of children's work that conveys specific elements or points. Teachers can reference specific work samples to anchor their questions and hypotheses in well-documented classroom activities.

Concerns about a specific child are best presented in the context of specific evidence. IEP team meetings for example, focused on a child who may be receiving special services, present opportunities to call upon classroom observations and other documentation that can contribute multiple perspectives to a team discussion. Classroom teachers and parents are the only members of an IEP team, for example, who can provide evidence of a child's daily functioning in the classroom and home environments (McAfee, Leong, & Bodrova, 2004).

Because of the increased pressures associated with high-stakes testing and accountability, the process of accurately and effectively reporting with other stakeholders has taken on greater significance. As teachers strive to present a child's skills and potential, they must assume responsibility for recording assessment data accurately, representing data with integrity, and linking assessment results to overarching theory and practices that are developmentally appropriate. Without evidence that supports children's development, administrative decisions may be based in the "head," more than the heart. Documentation of children's work conveys what is valued in a classroom or school, and illustrates, through use of explicit examples of children's work, the synergies between teaching and learning.

Legislators

"You're dealing with kids, and the principal is the first encounter a kid has with the justice system. Either it's a just system and the principal stands for justice, and he's going to get justice for you, or he's not" (S. Gould, personal communication, August 16, 2011). Legislators convey messages to the public that schools stand for something in our society. For children, families, and teachers who live in an American democratic society, school experiences do not always fit with the principles upon which the public education system was established.

> Democracy is messy. You have to work these things out. The state has it all
> wrong—the manner in which they're going about ratcheting up student
> achievement is anti-democratic. Engaging a community in the direction of a
> school isn't happening. The community is the best ally they have.
>
> (S. Gould, personal communication, August 16, 2011)

Legislators represent broader constituencies—groups of citizens—
invested in young children's learning. In efforts to secure classroom
environments that put children ahead of data collection and provide
resources based on need, and not success narrowly defined, educators
must be able to harness information gained through assessment of young
children and fight for policies that will serve children best.

Alfie Kohn, cited earlier in this book, is not shy about getting into the
mess, so to speak. In a recent article titled "Turning children into data: A
skeptic's guide to assessment programs" (Kohn, 2010), Kohn demonstrates his ability to get right to the point in the interest of bettering the
human condition, in this case, making sense of assessment data:

> If all the earnest talk about "data" (in the context of educating children) doesn't
> make you at least a little bit uneasy, it's time to recharge your crap detector.
> Most assessment systems are based on an outdated behaviorist model that
> assumes nearly everything can—and should—be quantified. But the more
> educators allow themselves to be turned into accountants, the more trivial their
> teaching becomes and the more their assessments miss.
>
> (p. 32)

As educators committed to working with children and families, we know
instinctively that children are more than mere numbers or data. The use
of meaningful assessment practices, and the ability to articulate and
communicate well the underlying philosophical and developmental
goals, will serve children and families well, and will provide a mirror for
educators to examine throughout their work. If assessment is about
telling a story, then it should read more like a novel than a dictionary. If
assessment is about putting puzzle pieces together to ensure equitable
practices for all young children, then educators have to develop strategies
akin to using all the straight-edged pieces first. Assessment should provide
the framework that holds the education picture, bringing it into focus.

Summary

Putting all of the assessment pieces together to build an informed picture
of children and their abilities is a complex task. Any attempts at assessment are enriched through collaboration with others, both to provide

insights and information as well as to provide alternative perspectives and interpretations. Evaluating data translates into written documents, reports, and communications with families and others. Enlisting family participation at the outset helps open lines of communication that will be helpful throughout a child's time in a particular classroom and school community. It also empowers families to act on behalf of their children in situations when they must advocate for what they feel is best. As educators consider the current culture of accountability and evidence-based programing, it is critical that they bear in mind the children who are represented by symbols and figures. As advocates for children and families in the education system, we all must continue to question mandates that feel uncomfortable and imagine policies that are child-centered and developmentally sound.

Now What?

1. How much autonomy should teachers have over the forms of communication they use to share information about children's progress? What considerations must they have in selecting appropriate forms of communication?
2. Describe assessment practices in the United States 20 years from today. What values, principles, and beliefs are at the core of these practices and why?
3. You are the mayor of a medium-size city. What actions would you take to ensure that assessment of young children is conducted in a meaningful way that includes qualitative as well as quantitative data? Who would you need to involve in your efforts?

Avenues for Inquiry

Yarp

This website provides a simple way for teachers to create surveys and questionnaires for families. The site is free, making access available to teachers and families who have the use of computers, and can open up lines of communication in innovative ways.

http://yarp.com

Department of Education

This link brings visitors to the Department of Education website and general index. Here you can find names of people to ask questions, voice concerns, or follow links about education reform efforts, NCLB, or other preK-12 initiatives. Twitter users can follow general information about the Department of Education at @usedgov, or can follow tweets from the US Department of Education press secretary Justin Hamilton at @EDPressSec.

    http://www2.ed.gov/about/contacts/gen/index.html

Teachers' Rights and Special Education

Teachers often worry about their responsibilities and legal responsibilities relating to the IEP process and subsequent implementation. This website was designed by an attorney to highlight the rights of regular teachers in Special Education. The site provides links to additional resources, publications, and organizations.

    http://www.adhd-add.info/teacherrights.html

9

Teacher as Researcher

Learning and teaching should not stand on opposite banks and just watch the river flow by; instead, they should embark together on a journey down the water. Through an active, reciprocal exchange, teaching can strengthen learning how to learn.

(Malaguzzi, 1998, p. 83)

We began this book focusing on the concepts of accountability and responsibility, and now, at the end of this particular journey, those concepts are important to consider in the context of teacher research, and new avenues to explore. As educators and practitioners, the more we learn about young children and their interests, the more questions tend to arise. The words *research* and *inquiry* are often used interchangeably, but there is a distinction made by Cochran-Smith & Lytle (2009) that is useful for the purposes of discussion in this chapter. Cochran-Smith & Lytle describe *inquiry* as a "somewhat softer word" than *research*, and underscore the idea that research is "not simply a beneficial, but benign, form of professional development," but "it is also a valuable mode of critique of the inequities in schools and society and of knowledge hierarchies" (p. ix).

"Recognizing that teachers and other practitioners are critical to the success of all efforts to improve education is clearly an idea whose time has come—or should have come long ago" (p. 1). Educators of young children benefit from learning alongside children and fellow educators, as well as from learning experiences that occur outside of the classroom. When we experience situations that are outside of our realms of experience and raise questions, our reactions to these situations "reveal the stance we take in the world as learners and as teachers" (Seidel, 2001, p. 330). Children have always observed how their teachers gather information and resources, as learners and consumers. In our current educational climate, pressures associated with accountability require teachers to do more than practice problem solving and information gathering—they must exhibit "best practices." When teachers seek insights or validation about new areas of understanding, they must also consider how their work and attitude can have a significant impact on children's attitudes and learning.

Assessment of young children affords educators many opportunities to pursue answers to questions that result from observations or other measures. Questions are at times specific to one child, and at other times directed at a small group of children. Assessment of the classroom environment may launch an investigation into different uses for classroom materials and innovative teaching practices and collaborative opportunities. "Genuine questions . . . and the curiosity that sparks their articulation mark the turning point when the act of teaching may become, simultaneously, an act of research" (Seidel, 2001, p. 331). Table 9.1 presents three crucial understandings about teachers as researchers.

When adults demonstrate positive attitudes toward learning and feel confident taking risks, they increase children's motivation to continue learning, as well as their own motivation. A solid understanding of child development and developmentally appropriate practices supports these inquisitive attitudes. A typical classroom climate that values questioning and curiosity about the world serves as a catalyst for teacher research, which naturally includes children, families, and colleagues in the process.

Ethics

From the teacher's point of view, it's her job to gather useful information that will guide and inform instruction. A guiding code of ethics provides educators with a supportive framework when grappling with choices and uncertainty related to student achievement and performance. There are already limited minutes in the day devoted to teaching and learning, so the moments spent assessing young children should be worthwhile and guide teachers' instruction in a valuable way. Educators and other practi-

Table 9.1 Three Crucial Understandings about Teachers as Researchers

- An understanding that teachers and children are active learners, collaborators, and coconspirators in the negotiation of curriculum.
- An understanding of the importance of observation, reflection, self-awareness, and interpretation as the foundation of learning in the classroom.
- An understanding of the documentation process as a cycle of inquiry involving questioning; observation; organization of data; analysis; interpretation and theory building; reframing of questions and assumptions; planning; and evaluation.

Source: Hill, Stremmel, & Fu (2005, p. 51).

tioners must be selective about their choice of assessments and use the information to teach and reach each child. Teachers can be bombarded with the latest and greatest assessment tools, but should be selective about which are used and for what purpose.

The National Association for the Education of Young Children (NAEYC) *Code of ethical conduct* (2005) specifies two ideals with respect to ethical responsibilities to children and assessment. They are fairly broad and make a lot of sense:

> I-1.6 To use assessment instruments and strategies that are appropriate for the children to be assessed, that are used only for the purposes for which they were designed, and that have the potential to benefit children.
>
> I-1.7 To use assessment information to understand and support children's development and learning, to support instruction, and to identify children who may need additional services.
>
> (p. 2)

Cause for Concern

Fortunately, young children are not assessed with great frequency in infant/toddler care and preschools, but this is slowly changing as more communities are bringing public preschool to their existing schools and seeking federal dollars to support programs and development. Educators are wary of an increase in public preschools because of the possibility of "pressures to push [assessment] practices down from elementary grades that are inappropriate for and even harmful to young children" (Mardell et al., 2010, p. 40). From an ethical standpoint, assessment should be a part of every day and embedded in instruction, changing what we know about our students as they grow and learn and, in turn, changing the curriculum and instruction. Using a variety of tools and methods to understand (or try to understand) children in a more complete way may be ideal, as no one assessment can provide teachers and families with the information they need to teach young children effectively.

When educators create opportunities to mine the meaning in ordinary classroom moments, they reduce the need for standardized assessments to inform them of children's capabilities. As discussed in Chapter 6, when children are given time and support for their play, teachers can learn a great deal about their abilities without having to administer a formal assessment or worry about high stakes outcomes. Children also need sufficient time to observe, to engage with peers and materials, to consider their strategies, to develop a plan, and to execute and revise their plans as they work toward mastery of social and academic situations. Adults control the degree to which they participate in a daily thinking process that provides time and space to make sense of the world. Children's school experiences should reflect the intentionality of teachers and administrators who recognize that

> children are by nature theory builders and meaning makers; they are in fact scientists, philosophers, and artists. And like scientists, philosophers, and artists, they simply must have long uninterrupted blocks of time to pursue their questions, to formulate and test their theories, to consider and reconsider their theories in light of conflicting or supporting data, to engage in dialogue and debate.
>
> (Gandini & Goldhaber, 2001, p. 139)

Practical Considerations

In a similar vein as the sentiment expressed in Chapter 8 that it takes a lot of keys to unlock understandings about children, a thoughtful combination of screening instruments, diagnostic measures, and informal assessments can be key to understanding what children know and what they need to be taught. This combination respects what is developmentally appropriate for children and helps ensure that assessment instruments are used in the way that they were designed, and for no other purpose.

A former principal wryly joked about an analogy between assessment and going to the hospital: "You're riding in the elevator with a broken leg, and you accidentally get off on the cardiology floor. Now you've got a heart problem!" (S. Gould, personal communication, August 16, 2011). Much like doctors use the tools they know best to assess an ailment, teachers use the tools they know best to assess children's learning. In keeping with the NAEYC ideals for ethical conduct, teachers must be careful not to misdiagnose problems that exist and diagnose problems that do not exist. Simply talking with colleagues brings issues to light for educators, who sometimes become so wrapped up and invested in their young students that they have trouble seeing what may be clear to others.

Using What We Know

Educators are becoming increasingly interested in looking for trends and tracking through school grades. Practices such as those included in systematic Response to Intervention (RTI) have influenced more ability grouping so that teachers can address issues with interventions more directly, in a group setting rather than merely one-on-one. It is interesting to notice trends, such as children who perform a certain way on a certain assessment in kindergarten, and then subsequently demonstrate similar behaviors in later grades. Done well, this type of foresight can help change the way teachers teach children in kindergarten to close the achievement gap for children in later grades. Done poorly, such assessment practices can label children and place them in groups that are virtually impossible to move from and which have as benchmarks and gateways specific scores on standardized measures.

Educator George Forman proposes that our education system do away with "the frequency count of general standards and henceforth search, document, and offer unique tags for any examples of high-level thinking" that teachers document among their students throughout all levels of public school. Forman argues that if educators dedicate their time and energy to the process of analyzing and articulating the unique attributes of a child, group of children, or even a school, we will have a much richer understanding of children's abilities than we obtain using standardized measures. He continues:

> And if we need to communicate this excellence to others, let them browse our indexed video database of evidence. If they don't have the time, ask them to take our word for it, which they do now with numbers that have no story. Taking our word for it, with access to video, is more intellectually honest and democratic than taking our numbers for it with no access to the examples that supported the judgment.
>
> (Forman, 2010, p. 35)

If the main purpose of assessment is to improve teaching and learning, then questions that originate as a result of simply observing children and reflecting on what happens in the classroom should be addressed in a similar spirit. The questions that spark noticing and wonderment, discussed in Chapter 1 (Why? Who? When? How? What?), can form the basis for investigation of specific classroom issues or problems, under the umbrella of teacher inquiry.

Inquiry

If we accept the distinction that Cochran-Smith & Lytle (2009) make between *research* and *inquiry*, then inquiry is a softer form of investigating what happens in classrooms with young children. If you are having trouble with the notion of softness, think *gentle* as opposed to rabbit fur or kitchen sponge. Since public education in the United States is linked to political and historical influences no matter how much people might wish to believe otherwise, it seems that both inquiry and research have the potential to shift the stance of educators from living in the known to embracing the ambiguous and uncertain. It is possible that foundations will fund a *research* proposal more readily than an *inquiry* project, but then we become trapped by conventions based on scientific biases, such as quantitative research being more rigorous than qualitative research and therefore more weighty and valuable, and teachers being practitioners distinct from researchers or scholars.

Embracing the unknown in inquiry stance can feel a bit uncomfortable and clumsy for teachers. Teachers recognize their role and responsibilities, which puts pressure on them to meet specific goals. Practices such as documentation of children's and teachers' learning therefore help to anchor moments of learning for further reflection, which makes a bit of room for teachers to do the work that is demanded of them, while simultaneously generating meaningful data.

Widening the Lens

In the book, *Teaching as inquiry* (2005), authors Hill, Stremmel, & Fu note that "collaborative activity, in which teaching and learning partners work together to design and carry out investigations on things that matter, forms the foundation of teacher research" (p. 44). When educators work together and with the children with whom they live and learn on a daily basis, they widen the lens through which they view ordinary, spontaneous moments of learning as well as purposeful, planned assessments. Widening the lens invites multiple perspectives and cognitive conflict, which at the very least exercises the brain. When educators investigate "things that matter," they open themselves up to awe as well as disequilibrium.

Assessment of young children provides insights into experiences that educators can design in an effort to help promote young children's development. Educators who are committed to children's healthy development can use their expertise and skills to build on the interests of young children in a spirit of inquiry that will promote children's

- amazement and appreciation for living things and the diversity of life;
- love of nature and a desire to care for the earth;
- interest in becoming contributing members of their family, class, and community;

- lifelong love of reading and an ability to communicate their thoughts through writing;
- appreciation for the arts and expressing themselves creatively;
- healthy, active lifestyles;
- positive approaches to learning;
- strong sense of self-worth as kind, loving, capable people who are able to solve problems;
- profound sense of wonder and true joy in learning (Jacobs & Crowley, 2010).

Trusting the Process

Educator Ben Mardell describes a wonderful example of teacher inquiry in his book, *From basketball to The Beatles* (1999). He immediately grabs readers' attention as he sets the scene that launched an investigation with his preschool class:

> My encounter with the dead squirrel started in complete innocence three days into my class's study of squirrels. As I was walking my son Sam to kindergarten, we came upon a deceased squirrel lying by the side of the road. A cursory examination revealed that the carcass was well preserved. Though I wasn't exactly sure what to do with it and despite some squeamishness about picking it up, I sensed the cadaver had potential as a teaching tool, so I scooped it into a shopping bag and, on my return home, popped it into the freezer.
>
> (Mardell, 1999, p. 1)

So many elements of that one simple, rich paragraph are noteworthy: Mardell's disposition and curiosity about the cadaver's "potential as a teaching tool"; his uncertainty about "what to do with it"; and his readiness to "scoop it into a shopping bag" and "pop it into the freezer." As Mardell embarked on a learning journey with his co-teacher, student teachers, and preschool class, the impulse to even consider the use of a dead squirrel is significant, for how many educators would choose a similar course of action today? Initiating and maintaining such a stance is hard work, requiring careful considerations of health and safety (physical and emotional), collaboration with teachers and families, and research with children and experts to follow lines of interest as they evolve. Many educators today are constrained by curricula that prescribe daily routines, lessons, and assessments, so the potential experiences that Mardell envisioned are out of the question in the minds of teachers and administrators. And yet the story Mardell shares in his book results in the accomplishment of many of the points above, described by Jacobs &

Figure 9.1 Dead Squirrel Playing

Crowley (2010)—such as appreciation for living things, love of nature and a desire to care for the earth, and a sense of wonder and true joy in learning.

There is an implicit level of trust in the learning process that is also important to mention. Assessment of young children informs instruction, which, in turn, influences the learning that teachers observe and record with young children. When teachers invest in a thoughtful process, they work to create a learning process that has many entry points and has staying power. The systematic use of documentation serves as a ruler and a compass for educators who engage in classroom investigations with young children. Teachers can measure the levels of students' engagement with content and concepts, and can also get a sense for where they can guide the group's learning with the use of gentle invitations or provocations to further inquiry.

A Cycle of Inquiry

Early childhood educators and advocates Gandini & Goldhaber (2001) describe the documentation process as one that extends teachers' "understanding of the concepts children are building, the theories they are constructing, and the questions they are posing" (p. 134). The process of documentation involves investment and trust in children's and teachers' learning of the sort described above. As a result of engaging in ongoing documentation that includes elements such as photographs, samples of students' work, snippets of children's and/or adults' dialogue, and video or audio tape, the group of learners evolves into a learning community. The documentation "challenges us to express our thinking articulately and publicly, and to accept the responsibility . . . to understand other points of view" (p. 134).

Gandini and Goldhaber propose a "spiraling cycle of inquiry" that involves the entire learning community in daily classroom explorations and engagement. While the individual elements in the cycle—framing early questions, observing, recording and collecting artifacts, organizing and analyzing the data, making early interpretations, reframing the questions, and responding (e.g. adapting materials) to the new understanding (e.g. planning)—are presented in a cyclical manner, the authors clarify that every process has a different trajectory (see Gandini & Goldhaber, 2001). Some processes build and grow in a progressive, cyclical manner, and other processes feel more stilted and elements in the cycle are encountered in a different sequence. The most important point is that the cycle of inquiry is much different than a linear process, and all configurations of collaboration among teachers and children are deeply embedded in the process and related documentation.

Because the process of inquiry and documentation is ongoing and evolving, the experiences of all participants are woven into the meaning making, which reflects individual personalities and hypotheses. As classroom curricula evolve to incorporate the outcomes of the group's inquiry process, documentation serves as both a spark and a touchstone for teachers and students. As you read the following case study, notice how the teachers and students delved into their own investigation into the winds of Honolulu. What evidence of learning do you see on the part of teachers and students, and how is documentation used to support and extend the group's inquiry?

Case Study: Wind Story/Learning Story

The "winds exercise" began when the preschool group was coming into the classroom from the playground one day, and a strong wind blew. One child asked, "What kind of wind was that?" This became the question for one of their group meetings. At the beginning of the year, Leslie and Margaret had decided to use questions beginning with "I wonder . . ." to provoke the children's thinking, so here was an opportunity to ask the group, "I wonder what kind of wind just blew on us?" To the teachers' amazement, as the children shared their thinking about the winds, they came up with 18 different winds, such as: a tornado wind, Japanese wind, windy-wind, summer wind, school wind (which later shifted to an everywhere/McDonald's wind), leaf wind, house wind, tree wind that blows the kites hard (this became kite wind), a mountain wind, winter wind (became the sea wind), storm wind, flower wind, pool wind, snow wind, fire wind, winter wind (shifted to monster/ghost wind), rose wind, and air wind.

"I think we have a hot subject," Leslie thought. "This could be our next project!"

***

The teachers wanted to know more about what the children knew about winds. Had they made up those names for the winds in the moment, for the sake of the group discussion, or were the winds based on actual observations the children had experienced? The next day, the teachers decided, "Let's step it up and make them take more risks—describe 18 different *sounds*." Leslie and Margaret knew that the children knew something about winds, so they all began observing winds closely. The children were able to share 18 different sounds that were associated with their own winds. The teachers continued to explore what the children knew about winds in their group discussions. As individual children shared their knowledge about the winds, the group began to shape a collective identity as explorers and collaborators in search of understanding. The teachers, as co-learners, joined in the construction of knowledge with the children. Such a partnership with the preschoolers laid a safe foundation for the children to feel confident taking risks and articulating their unique ideas.

***

The teachers were captivated by the children's knowledge and expertise. They decided to explore the winds further as a group, and created a new kind of group meeting—Project Meetings—where they followed a protocol of children presenting their work, their theories, and then children could ask questions and give feedback. During the Project Meetings the group took the next risk—*drawing the winds*. As the project kept moving, the class took research trips through the fields where they first found the winds.

Leslie shared, "What was amazing was that some parents came along and saw how we let the children learn on their own rather than giving them the information ahead of time.

The girl who'd first mentioned the winds had a mom who was an oceanographer. She came in to look at the kids' drawings of the winds and said the kids were dead on. Their own experience was what was so crucial, rather than someone filling them up. The children's observations were validated."

***

As extraordinary as the group's ideas and explanations were, the teachers sensed some frustration on the children's part that they couldn't quite capture the movement of their winds in a static drawing. They grappled with ideas about how to make the children's theories move, perhaps using a different medium.

The teachers inquired about ways for the children to visualize the winds. The preschool group entered into collaboration with animators—high school animation students and their technology teacher. The preschoolers went to the tech lab from time to time to work with the computer animation system. The high school students' task was to translate the children's drawings into an animated version of their winds. The preschoolers drew their winds directly into the computer, and the animators added the visual movement. Then the children revised their theories and ideas. For example, one child noticed that a flag wasn't waving the right way in the animated version of his wind.

The teachers wondered if and when they should give the children the technical names for the winds, but decided that it was better to let the learning unfold. They eventually gave the children the technical names at certain times and let the children be the ones to determine whether or not to give them the "right" names.

***

Throughout the project, Leslie and Margaret assessed the children's learning. "We used the 'learning stories' format from Margaret Carr and seven to eight classroom philosophy statements, and a list of learning dispositions," Leslie explained. They also used video and still photos, and shared information with families through their class website. "These daily 'light' assessments (something a child did during the day) help parents see that teachers are looking closely at children's learning everyday, as ongoing, embedded, assessment." Leslie continued, "The statements children make are so great, and not just for accreditation. It tells us that the kids are ready to move into kindergarten and makes meaning for our program. This is what I communicate with families."

Leslie reflected on the wind projects, "The kids would've missed so many things if we had been more direct with our teaching. They were reading each other's lines on the paper, and discussing the lines, saying things like, 'That doesn't make sense.'"

***

The children made a "wind book" as a gift for Leslie at the end of that year. "Now, new classes of children who know nothing about it look at the book and find inspiration. Some wind catchers we made are still up in the yard. The new generations find continual inspiration," Leslie reflected. Leslie shared an example of a little girl sitting cross-legged on a picnic table, holding the wind book. She was looking down on Honolulu, waiting for the wind described in the book, and her eyes lit up as the "windy-wind" started moving up the mountain, beginning with the pine trees. Another child learned from the wind book that if you go across a certain valley, by the extinct volcano, the wind will behave a certain way.

Leslie explained, "Teachers come into a classroom with pre-conceived ideas about the way things should be. In our case, the teachers experienced just as much wonder as the kids in the moment."

Partners in the Process

As seen in the Wind Story/Learning Story, the relationships that exist between teachers and children benefit from communication between all active participants, but the "primary beneficiary is always and above all else the child, who will be gaining the maximum advantage from this atmosphere of dialogue (Rinaldi, 2006, p. 45). Teachers and children are natural partners in the processes of research and inquiry, and everyday noticings that can be recorded through various means and shared with a classroom or school community. Throughout this book you have read descriptions of partnerships that exist in and among early childhood classrooms, higher education settings, and professional education communities. The following example illustrates a school-wide investigation that resulted in many positive benefits for children and educators, alike.

Zooms

"A Zoom is a three- by four-foot documentation panel that offers a close look, as with a zoom lens, at the children's and teachers' responses and understandings of their classrooms' research question (Mardell et al., 2009, p. 4). For six educators at the Eliot-Pearson Children's School, constructing Zooms was the focus of their joint investigation into new understandings about the children in their classrooms and their teaching practices. The research question guiding the group's inquiry was: How can focusing on a particular moment of classroom life help teachers understand children's capabilities and concerns and support their collaborations with peers?

Zooms are documentation panels—documentation of the sort described throughout this book—that include images (e.g. photographs, samples of children's artwork) and words (e.g. quotes from discussions among children, among teachers, and between children and teachers) representing ideas created as a result of the inquiry. Over the course of an academic year, the six educators documented daily teaching and learning experiences and ordinary classroom interactions. While the physical creation and presentation of the Zooms marked the conclusion of the formal schoolwide inquiry process, the public display of Zooms ignited conversations between children, families, and teachers at the school, as well as with colleagues at other schools and universities.

The initial explicit goal of the Zooms was to identify and illustrate fundamental elements that were so critical to the evolution of relationships and understandings between members of the school community as they encountered the inquiry question head-on or indirectly, through ordinary classroom activity. A fortunate byproduct of the research was the creation of what the teachers identified as a professional learning community—"a culture of inquiry in their early childhood school that also enhanced staff collegiality. The teachers evolved from individual, reflective practitioners to collaborative, schoolwide teacher researchers" (Mardell et al., 2009, p.1).

Engaging Families

The Zooms experience brought parents and families into the schoolwide inquiry process, which is a welcome invitation for many families who feel a sense of disconnect with their children's public education. From a historical perspective, responsibility for schools has shifted over the decades from local responsibility to state responsibility, and this is accepted as part of our country's political history. However, the shift in financial responsibility for public schools also meant that the control over school decisions shifted from the local community to state agencies. "The result has been a loss of control and sense of responsibility for schools at the local level for all persons involved in the school, but especially parents" (Olsen & Fuller, 2008, pp. 217–18). The perceived distance between parents and schools has only increased as high-stakes accountability efforts have taken root in the educational system.

An example of a collaboration that combines assessment and family-engagement efforts in the interest of children's successful, healthy development is the Three-to-Third initiative in Boston. The Harvard Graduate School of Education, the Boston public schools, and the Boston Mayor's office join forces in this innovative effort to reduce achievement gaps between children of different racial, ethnic, and socioeconomic backgrounds.

This initiative supports several Boston schools in a number of family-engagement activities. For example, children receive weekly reading logs that request families to read to their children at least four times a week. Teacher home visits occur twice a year, and family-literacy events are sponsored in schools and in the greater community. One interesting element of this initiative is how participation in these activities is monitored and how responsibility is shared. Schools are responsible for monitoring how many families complete their weekly reading logs, receive home visits, and attend family-literacy events. School principals are therefore responsible for using this data to hold themselves accountable for supporting and promoting the initiative. As schools collect data over time, they will be able to observe trends in progress and obstacles, identify improvements, and focus their efforts (Weissbourd, Weissbourd, & O'Carroll, 2010).

Educators know that "outcomes typically don't change unless programs are highly intentional and laserlike in their focus, closely linking strategies and activities to outcomes" (ibid., p. 115). Collaborative assessment is one way to engage families in the efforts to educate and inspire young children. As teachers delve into close examinations of student work and their own teaching practices, they create a foundation from which they can take risks and model dispositions that children and families can learn from.

If children are to develop a lifelong love of learning and participate fully in society as engaged citizens, then the seeds planted in early childhood will thrive in an environment that nurtures passion for learning and trust in the learning process. The joy that is a fundamental right for all children should not be stowed in a cubby when the classroom day begins, along with books and home toys. It must be celebrated and included in assessment processes that honor and celebrate the whole child.

Summary

Teachers engage in research when they follow their curiosity to learn more about children—their interests and their abilities—and elements of their own teaching. The processes of inquiry and more formal research reveal much about children's knowledge of concepts and their skills related to specific domains. As responsible educators, it is important to consider ethical ideals that teachers are bound by in their work with young children. Recognizing the developmental appropriateness of assessment and research is fundamental to practices that protect children from less than ideal classroom activity and, in the worst case, harm. Examples of teacher research and initiatives provide inspiration for practitioners who wish to engage children, families, and colleagues in meaningful inquiry efforts.

Now What?

1. Describe an ideal strategy for teachers to engage families in classroom inquiry. How can children, families, and teachers feel valued as members of the learning community?
2. Gandini & Goldhaber (1991) propose a cycle of inquiry that incorporates documentation as a fundamental tool for teachers and children. Why is the cycle of inquiry an effective way for teachers to frame their inquiry process?
3. What are some ways that our society might recognize the importance of teacher research in young children's development?

Avenues for Inquiry

Leslie Gleim's Preschool Class

This website features Leslie Gleim's preschool class at Mid Pacific Institute in Honolulu, HI. Leslie posts reflections and stories about the class's projects and related experiences.
   http://www.midpac.edu/elementary/PG

Animated Winds

The following websites link visitors to examples of animation that preschoolers made to bring their winds to life. Other examples are available on youtube.com:

Summer wind:
http://www.youtube.com/user/mpitechteacher#p/u/8/Lkl7TI83AAo
Storm wind:
http://www.youtube.com/user/mpitechteacher#p/u/4/xYfJx4Bhtik

Learning Stories

This website provides examples of Learning Stories that invite discussion among educators interested in using narratives to assess and celebrate children's learning. The creator of the Learning Stories provides some insights into the process and development of these stories.

http://earlylearningstories.info/

Bibliography

Assouline, S.G., & Lupkowski-Shoplik, A. (2005). *Developing math talent*. Austin, TX: Prufrock Press.

Bagnato, S.J. (2009). *Authentic assessment for early childhood intervention: Best practices*. New York: The Guilford Press.

Benjamin, W. (1999). *The arcades project*. Translated by H. Eiland & K. McLaughlin. Cambridge, MA: Harvard University Press.

Bergen, D. (2009). Play as the learning medium for future scientists, mathematicians, and engineers. *American Journal of Play*, 413–428.

Berman, S. (2010, September). The achievement gap vs. the empowerment gap. *Citizenship Matters*. Denver, CO: Education Commission of the States.

Blythe, T., Allen, D., & Powell, B.S. (2007). *Looking together at student work, 2/e*. New York: Teachers College Press.

Bodrova, E., & Leong, D.J. (2007). *Tools of the mind: The Vygotskian approach to early childhood education*. Upper Saddle River, NJ: Merrill/Pearson.

Borich, G.D. (2011). *Observation skills for effective teaching, 6/e*. Boston, MA: Pearson.

Boris-Schacter, S. (2001, March 7). The politics and practice of student assessment: Classroom contradictions. *Education Week*, 20(25):42–43.

Bronfenbrenner, U. (1979). *The ecology of human development: Experiments by nature and design*. Cambridge, MA: Harvard University Press.

Bullard, J. (2010). *Creating environments for learning: Birth to age 8*. Upper Saddle River, NJ: Merrill.

Carlsson-Paige, N. (2008). *Taking back childhood: Helping your kids thrive in a fast-paced, media-saturated, violence-filled world*. New York: Penguin Books.

Cavanagh, S. (2011, April 6). Excessive testing focus saps love of learning, Korean ex-official says. *Education Week*, 30(27):18.

Center for Applied Special Technology (CAST). (2011). *Universal design for learning guidelines version 2.0*. Wakefield, MA: Author.

Chawla, L. (1990). Ecstatic places. *Children's environments quarterly*, 7(4):18–23.

Chen, J., & McNamee, G.D. (2007). *Bridging: Assessment for teaching and learning in early childhood classrooms, prek-3*. Thousand Oaks, CA: Corwin Press.

Chen, D.W., Nimmo, J., & Fraser, H. (2009). Becoming a culturally responsive early childhood educator: A tool to support reflection by teachers embarking on the anti-bias journey. *Multicultural Perspectives*, 11(2):101–106.

Cobb, C.L., Danby, S., & Farrell, A. (2005). Governance of children's everyday spaces. *Australian Journal of Early Childhood*, 30(1):14–20.

Cochran-Smith, M., & Lytle, Susan L. (2009). *Inquiry as stance: Practitioner research for the next generation*. New York: Teachers College Press.

Coleman-Kiner, A. (2011, June 8). Leading with love. *Education Week*, 30(33):25.

Copple, C., & Bredekamp, S. (Eds.). (2009). *Developmentally appropriate practice in early childhood programs serving children from birth through age 8 (3/e)*. Washington, DC: National Association for the Education of Young Children.

Council of Chief State School Officers. (2010, July). Interstate Teacher Assessment and Support Consortium (InTASC). *Model core teaching standards: a resource for state dialogue (draft for public comment).* Washington, DC: Author.

Darling-Hammond, L. (2010). *The flat world and education: How America's commitment to equity will determine our future.* New York: Teachers College Press.

Derman-Sparks, L., & Edwards, J.O. (2010). *Anti-bias curriculum for young children and ourselves.* Washington, DC: NAEYC.

Dewey, J. (1916). *Democracy and education.* New York: Macmillan.

Dewey, J. (1910/1933). *How we think: A restatement of the relation of reflective thinking to the educative process.* Lexington, MA: Heath.

Diana School. (1990). *In viaggio coi diritti dei bambini.* [A journey into the rights of children.] Booklet published by the school and republished by Reggio Children S.r.l. (1995). Distributed by Reggio Children USA, Washington, DC.

Edwards, C.P., Gandini, L., & Forman, G.E. (1998). *The hundred languages of children: The Reggio Emilia approach—advanced reflections.* Greenwich, CT.: Ablex Publishing Corporation.

Elkind, D. (2001, May). Thinking about children's play. *Child Care Information Exchange,* 27–28.

Elkind, D. (2007). *The power of play: How spontaneous, imaginative activities lead to happier, healthier children.* Cambridge, MA: De Capo Press.

Espinosa, L. (2010). *Getting it right for young children from diverse backgrounds: Applying research to improve practice.* Washington, DC: NAEYC.

Essex, N.L. (2006). *What every teacher should know about No Child Left Behind.* New York: Pearson.

Felstiner, S. (2004, May/June). Emergent environments: Involving children in classroom design. *Child Care Information Exchange,* 41–43.

Finchler, J. (2000). *Testing Miss Malarkey.* New York: Walker & Company.

Fiore, L.B., & Rosenquest, B. (Winter 2010). Shifting the culture of higher education: Influences on students, teachers, and pedagogy. *Theory into Practice,* 49(1): 14–20.

Folbre, N. (2011, June 20). Will business buy into early childhood education? *The New York Times.*

Forman, G. (2010). Documentation and accountability: The shift from numbers to indexed narratives. *Theory into Practice,* 49(1): 29–35.

Froebel, F. (1912). Froebel's chief writings on education. Retrieved 25 July from http://core.roehampton.ac.uk/digital/froarc/frochi

Galvin, M. (2007). Implementing Response to Intervention (RTI): Considerations for practitioners. *Great Lakes West Newsletter.* Chicago, IL: Learning Points Associates.

Gandini, L. (1998). Educational and caring spaces. *The hundred languages of children: The Reggio Emilia approach—advanced reflections, 2/e.* Westport, CT: Ablex Publishing, 161–178.

Gandini, L., & Goldhaber, J. (1991). Two reflections about documentation. In L. Gandini & C.P. Edwards (Eds.), *Bambini: The Italian approach to infant/toddler care.* New York: Teachers College Press, 124–145.

Gardner, H. (1983). *Frames of mind: The theory of multiple intelligences.* New York: Basic Books.

Given, H., Kuh, L., LeeKeenan, D., Mardell, B., Redditt, S., & Twombly, S. (2010). Changing school culture: Using documentation to support collaborative inquiry. *Theory into Practice,* 49(1):36–46.

Gonzalez-Mena, J. (2008). *Diversity in early care and education: Honoring differences, 5/e.* Washington, DC: NAEYC.

Gross, R., & Gross, B. (Eds.). (1969). *Radical school reform.* New York: Simon & Schuster.

Hainstock, E. (1986). *The essential Montessori.* New York: Plume.

Haney, W. (2006). *Evidence on education under NCLB (and how Florida boosted NAEP scores and reduced the race gap).* Paper presented at the Hechinger Institute "Broad Seminar for K-12 Reporters," Teachers College, Columbia University, New York, September 8–10.

Hawkins, D. (1967). *The informed vision on learning and human nature.* New York: Agathon Press.

Heckman, J.J., & Masterov, D.V. (2007). *The productivity argument for investing in young children.* T.W. Schultz Award Lecture at the Allied Social Sciences Association annual meeting, Chicago, IL, January 5–7. Retrieved August 2011 from http://jenni.uchicago.edu/human-inequality/papers/Heckman_final_all_wp_2007-03-22c_jsb.pdf

Hill, L.T., Stremmel, A.J., & Fu, V.R. (2005). *Teaching as inquiry: Rethinking curriculum in early childhood education.* Boston: Allyn & Bacon.

Hilliard, D. (2011). Making families welcome. *Environments: A beginnings workshop book.* Redmond, WA: Exchange Press, Inc., 44–45.

Jacobs, G., & Crowley, K. (2010). *Reaching standards and beyond in kindergarten: nurturing children's sense of wonder and joy in learning.* Thousand Oaks, CA: Corwin.

John, A., & Wheway, R. (2004). *Can play will play: Disabled children and access to outdoor playgrounds.* London: National Playing Fields Association.

Jones, E., & Nimmo, J. (1994). *Emergent curriculum.* Washington, DC: NAEYC.

Jones, S.M., Brown, J.L., & Aber, L. (2011, March/April). Two-year impacts of a universal school-based social-emotional and literacy intervention: An experiment in translational developmental research. *Child Development,* 82(2):533–554.

Kagan, S.L., & Kauerz, K. (2011, July 13). The race to the top—early learning challenge: Moving the agenda. *Education Week,* 30(36):43, 48.

Kastner, M. (2011, May 11). Testing the test. *Education Week,* 30(30):40.

Kelleher, M. (2011, March 2) Some parents remain leery of RTI's benefits. *Education Week,* 30(22), s14, s15.

Kelly-Vance, L., & Ryalls, B.O. (2005). Best practices in play assessment and intervention. *Best Practices in School Psychology V,* 33(2):549–560.

Kim, D., & Huynh, H. (2010). Equivalence of paper-and-pencil and online administration modes of the statewide English test for students with and without disabilities. *Educational Assessment,* 15(2):107–121.

Kirp, D.L. (2011). *Kids first: Five big ideas for transforming children's lives and America's future.* New York: Public Affairs.

Kohn, A. (2001). Fighting the test: Turning frustration into action. *Phi Delta Kappan,* 82(5):348–358.

Kohn, A. (2010, August 25). Turning children into data: A skeptic's guide to assessment programs, *Education Week,* 30(1):29, 32.

Kohn, A. (2011, April 27). Poor teaching for poor children . . . in the name of school reform. *Education Week,* 30(29):32–34.

Kozol, J. (1991). *Savage inequalities: Children in America's schools.* New York: HarperCollins.

Krechevsky, M. (1991). Project Spectrum: An innovative assessment alternative. *Educational Leadership,* 48(5):43–48.

Krechevsky, M., & Mardell, B. (2001). Four features of learning in groups. In *Making learning visible: Children as individual and group learners.* Reggio Emilia, Italy: Reggio Children srl, 278–283.

Krechevsky, M., Rivard, M., & Burton, F. (Winter 2010). Accountability in three realms: Making learning visible inside and outside the classroom. *Theory into Practice,* 49 (1). Mahwah, NJ: Lawrence Erlbaum Associates, Inc., 64–71.

Ladson-Billings, G. (2001). *Crossing over to Canaan: The journey of new teachers in diverse classrooms.* San Francisco: Jossey-Bass.

Lester, S., & Russell, W. (2010). Children's right to play: An examination of the importance of play in the lives of children worldwide. *Working Paper No. 57.* The Hague, The Netherlands: Bernard van Leer Foundation.

Levin, D. (2003). Beyond banning war and superhero play: Meeting children's needs in violent times. *Young Children,* 58(3): 60–63.

Louv, R. (2005). *Last child in the woods: Saving our children from nature-deficit disorder.* Chapel Hill, NC: Algonquin Books of Chapel Hill.

McAfee, O., Leong, D.J., & Bodrova, E. (2004). *Basics of assessment: A primer for early childhood educators.* Washington, D.C.: NAEYC.

Malaguzzi, L. (1998). History, ideas, and basic philosophy: An interview with Lella Gandini. In C. Edwards, L. Gandini & G. Forman (Eds.), *The hundred languages of children, 2/e,* 49–77. Ablex Publishing, Westport, CT.

Mardell, B. (1999). *From basketball to The Beatles: In search of compelling early childhood curriculum.* Portsmouth, NH: Heinemann.

Mardell, B., Fiore, L., Boni, M., & Tonachel, M. (2010). The rights of children: Policies to best serve three-, four- and five-year-olds in public schools. *Journal of the Scholarship of Teaching and Learning,* 5(1): 37–52.

Mardell, B., LeeKeenan, D., Given, H., Robinson, D., Merino, B., & Liu-Constant, Y. (2009). Zooms: Promoting schoolwide inquiry and improving practice. *Voices of Practitioners,* 11:1–15.

Marisco Institute for Early Learning & Literacy (MIELL) (2010). *The case against testing young children to evaluate teacher effectiveness: A position statement from the Marisco Institute for Early Learning and Literacy, Issue Brief No. 4.* Denver, CO: University of Denver.

Marisco Institute for Early Learning & Literacy (2003). *Guidelines for preschool learning experiences.* Malden, MA: Author.

Meisels, S.J., Marsden, D.B., Jablon, J.R., Dorfman, A.B., & Dichtelmiller, M.K. (2001). *The work sampling system.* Upper Saddle River, NJ: Pearson Education.

Miller, E., & Almon, J. (2009). *Crisis in the kindergarten: Why children need to play in school.* College Park, MD: Alliance for Childhood.

Mitchell, S., Foulger, T.S., & Wetzel, K. (2009). Ten tips for involving families through Internet-based communication. *Young Children,* 64(5):46–49.

Montessori, M. (1964). *The Montessori method.* New York: Schocken Books.

Montessori, M. (1965). *Dr. Montessori's own handbook.* New York: Schocken Books.

Montessori, M. (1967). *The absorbent mind.* New York: Dell Publishing Co.

Nathan, L.F. (2009). *The hardest questions aren't on the test: Lessons from an innovative urban school.* Boston, MA: Beacon Press.

National Association for the Education of Young Children (NAEYC) (2003). *Early childhood curriculum, assessment, and program evaluation: Building an effective, accountable system in programs for children birth through 8.* Washington, DC: NAEYC.

National Association for the Education of Young Children (NAEYC) (2005). *Code of ethical conduct and statement of commitment: Position statement of the National Association for the Education of Young Children.* Washington, D.C.: NAEYC.

National Association of School Psychologists (2005). *Position statement on early childhood assessment.* Bethesda, MD: Author.

National Board for Professional Teaching Standards (NBPTS) (2001a). *The impact of National Board Certification on teachers: A survey of National Board Certified Teachers and assessors.* Arlington, VA: Author.

National Center on Response to Intervention (NCRTI) (2010, March). *Essential components of RTI—A closer look at Response to Intervention.* Washington, DC: U.S. Department of Education, Office of Special Education Programs, National Center on Response to Intervention.

National Scientific Council on the Developing Child (NSCDC) (2004). Young children develop in an environment of relationships. Working Paper No. 1. Retrieved July 25, 2011 from http://www. developingchild.net

Neugebauer, B. (Ed.) (2011). *Environments: A beginning workshop book.* Redmond, WA: Exchange Press, Inc.

Obama, B. (2011). *A blueprint for reform: The reauthorization of the Elementary and Secondary Education Act—A letter from the President.* Retrieved August 5, 2011 from http://www2.ed.gov/policy/elsec/leg/blueprint/publication_pg2.html

Olds, A. (2001). *Child care design guide.* New York: McGraw-Hill.

Olsen, G., & Fuller, M.L. (2008). *Home-school relations: Working successfully with parents and families, 3/e.* Boston: Allyn & Bacon.

Paley, V.G. (1997). *The girl with the brown crayon.* Cambridge, MA: Harvard University Press.

Park, B. (2009). *Junie B.'s essential survival guide to school.* New York: Random House, Inc.

Parr, J.M., & Timperley, H. (2008). Teachers, schools, and using evidence: Considerations of preparedness. *Assessment in Education: Principles, Policy, & Practice,* 15(1):57–71.

Parten, M.B. (1932). Social participation among preschool children. *Journal of Abnormal and Social Psychology,* 27:243–269.

Pellis, S., & Pellis, V. (2006). Play and the development of social engagement. In P. Marshall & N. Fox (eds.), *The Development of Social Engagement.* New York: Oxford University Press.

Pelo, A. (2011). From borders to bridges: Transforming our relationships with parents. *Environments: A beginnings workshop book*. Redmond, WA: Exchange Press, Inc., 37–40.

Piaget, J. (1947/1962). *Play, dreams, and imitation in early childhood*. London: Routledge.

Pratt, C. (1948). *I learn from children: An adventure in progressive education*. New York: Simon & Schuster.

Punch, S. (2003). Childhoods in the majority world: Miniature adults or tribal children? *Sociology*, 37(2):277–295.

Ravitch, D. (2010). *The death and life of the great American school system: How testing and choice are undermining education*. New York: Basic Books.

Ready to Learn Providence & Project Zero. (2011). *Places to play in Providence: A guide to the city by our youngest citizens*. Retrieved July 25, 2011 from http://issuu.com/r2lp/docs/places_to_play_in_pvd

Rebora, A. (2010). Uncovering the 'invisible barriers' to student success. *Teacher Magazine*. Retrieved August 3, 2011 from http://www.edweek.org/tm/articles/2010/06/07/lindanathanbb.html

Rhodes, R.L., Ochoa, S.H., & Ortiz, S.O. (2005). *Assessing culturally and linguistically diverse students: A practical guide*. New York: The Guilford Press.

Riddile, M. (2010, December 15). PISA: It's poverty not stupid. *The Principal Difference*. Retrieved July 15, 2011 from http://nasspblogs.org/principaldifference/2010/12/pisa_its_poverty_not_stupid_1.html

Rinaldi, C. (2001). Documentation and assessment: What is the relationship? In *Making learning visible: Children as individual and group learners*. Reggio Emilia, Italy: Reggio Children srl, 78–89.

Rinaldi, C. (2006). *In dialogue with Reggio Emilia: Listening, researching, and learning*. New York: Routledge.

Robinson, K. (2009). *TED and Redditt asked Sir Ken Robinson anything—and he answered*. Retrieved August 3, 2011 from http://blog.ted.com/2009/08/12/ted_and_reddit_1/

Salvia, J., Ysseldyke, J., & Bolt, S. (2009). *Assessment in special and inclusive education, 11/e*. Belmont, CA: Wadsworth Cengage.

Samuels, C.A. (2011, March 2). RTI: An approach on the march. *Education Week*, 30(22), s2–s5.

Sandseter, E.B.H., & Kennair, L.E.O. (2011). Children's risky play from an evolutionary perspective: The anti-phobic effects of thrilling experiences. *Evolutionary Psychology*, 9(2):257–284.

Scheinfeld, D.R., Haigh, K.M., & Scheinfeld, S.J.P. (2008). *We are all explorers: Learning and teaching with Reggio principles in urban settings*. New York: Teachers College Press.

Schmoker, M., & Graff, G. (2011, April 20). More argument, fewer standards. *Education Week*, 30(28):31, 33.

Schwartz, R.B., Levin, B., & Gamoran, A. (2001, April 6). Learning from abroad. *Education Week*, 30(27):34–36.

Schweinhart, L., Barnes, H., & Weikart, D. (1993). *Significant benefits: The High/Scope Perry Preschool study through age 27*. Ypsilanti, MI: High/Scope Press.

Scott, J.C. (1998). *Seeing like a state: How certain schemes to improve the human condition have failed*. New Haven, CT: Yale University Press.

Segura-Mora, A. (2008). What color is beautiful? In A. Pelo (Ed.), *Rethinking Early Childhood Education*. Milwaukee, WI: Rethinking Schools, Ltd.

Seidel, S. (2001). To be part of something bigger than oneself. In *Making learning visible: Children as individual and group learners*. Reggio Emilia, Italy: Reggio Children srl, 312–321.

Seidel, S. (2001). "The question cannot be satisfied with waiting": Perspectives on research in education. In *Making learning visible: Children as individual and group learners*. Reggio Emilia, Italy: Reggio Children srl, 330–334.

Shermis, M.D., & DiVesta, F.J. (2011). *Classroom assessment in action*. Lanham, MD: Rowman & Littlefield Publishers.

Snow, C.E., & Van Hemel, S.B. (2008). *Early childhood assessment: Why, what, and how*. Washington, D.C.: National Academies Press.

Sparks, S.D. (2011, June 8). Panel finds few learning benefits in high-stakes exams. *Education Week*, 30(33):1, 14.

Stagnitti, K. (2004). Understanding play: The implications for play assessment. *Australian Occupational Therapy Journal*, 51:3–12.

Strozzi, P. (2001). Daily life at school: Seeing the extraordinary in the ordinary. In *Making learning visible: Children as individual and group learners.* Reggio Emilia, Italy: Reggio Children srl, 58–77.

Tishman, S., Perkins, D.N., & Jay, E. (1995). *The thinking classroom: Learning and teaching in a culture of thinking.* Boston: Allyn & Bacon.

Turner, T., & Wilson, D.G. (Winter 2010). Reflections on documentation: A discussion with thought leaders from Reggio Emilia. *Theory Into Practice,* 49(1):5–13.

United Nations Convention on the Rights of the Child. (1989). UN General Assembly Document A/RES/44/25 *USA IPA.* Retrieved July 25, 2011 from http://www.ipausa.org/ipadeclaration.html

United States Department of Education (1977). Individuals with Disabilities Education Act of 1977, Public Law No. 94-142.

United States Department of Education (1994). Improving America's Schools Act of 1994, Public Law No. 103-382.

Vecchi, V. (2010). *Art and creativity in Reggio Emilia: Exploring the role and potential of ateliers in early childhood education.* New York: Routledge.

Vogell, H. (2011, July 6). Investigation into APS cheating finds unethical behavior across every level. *The Atlanta Journal-Constitution.* Retrieved July 6, 2011 from http://www.ajc.com/news/investigation-into-aps-cheating-1001375.html

Weller, S., & Bruegel, I. (2009). Children's 'place' in the development of neighbourhood social capital. *Urban Studies,* 46(3):629–643.

Weissbourd, B., Weissbourd, R., & O'Carroll, K. (2010). Family engagement. In V. Washington and J.D. Andrews (Eds.), *Children of 2010: Creating a Better Tomorrow.* Washington, D.C.: NAEYC, 114–118.

Wiggins, G. (2011). *Grant Wiggins: Defining assessment.* Retrieved 25 July, 2011 from http://www.edutopia.org/grant-wiggins-assessment

Wilson, D.M., & Weiner, R. (2001, October 10). Education called key to defense. *[Rockland County, NY] Journal News,* B1.

Wilson, P. (2009). *The Playwork Primer.* College Park, MD: Alliance for Childhood.

Wohlwend, K. (2005). Chasing friendship: Acceptance, rejection, and recess play. *Childhood Education,* 81(22):77.

Wolk, R.A. (2011, March 9). Standards-based accountability's high stakes. *Education Week,* 30(23): 24, 32.

Xueqin, J. (2010, December 8). The test Chinese schools still fail: High scores for Shanghai's 15-year-olds are actually a sign of weakness. *The Wall Street Journal Asia.* Retrieved August 4, 2011 from http://online.wsj.com/article/SB10001424052748703766704576008692493038646.html

Index